ET TU, JUDAS?
Then Fall Jesus!

ET TU, JUDAS?
Then Fall Jesus!

Gary Courtney

iUniverse, Inc.

New York Lincoln Shanghai

ET TU, JUDAS? *Then Fall Jesus!*

iUniverse, Inc.

For information address:
iUniverse, Inc.
2021 Pine Lake Road, Suite 100
Lincoln, NE 68512
www.iuniverse.com

Cover illustration—Detail of *The Death of Caesar,* from the workshop of Apollonio di Giovanni (Courtesy of the Ashmolean Museum)

First Published 1992. Reprinted 2004

ISBN 0 646 08733 9

ISBN: 0-595-32868-7 (pbk)
ISBN: 0-595-77790-2 (cloth)

Printed in the United States of America

He that answereth a matter before he heareth it
It is a folly and shame unto him—Proverbs 18:13

Frequently occurring abbreviations and notes:

AJ—The *Jewish Antiquities* by Josephus.
App *CW*—The *Civil Wars* in Appianus' Roman History.
BJ—The *Jewish Wars* by Josephus.
Dio *RH*—Roman History by Cassius Dio Cocceianus.
DJ—*Divus Julius* by Stefan Weinstock.
Jn—The Gospel of John.
KJV—The King James bible.
Lk—The Gospel of Luke.
Mk—The Gospel of Mark.
Mt—The Gospel of Matthew.
NT—New Testament.
OT—Old Testament.
Plut—Plutarchus' *Lives*.
SS—The "Suffering Servant" of Isaiah 52:13–53:12.
Suet—Gaius Suetonius Tranquillus.
Suet *JC*—The chapter on *The Deified Julius*, in Suetonius' *The Twelve Caesars*.

In this book I have generally followed the English model of spelling rather than the US one. Some of the idiom is Australian. All emphasised or parenthesised sections in the citations are mine unless otherwise indicated.

Gary Courtney

Contents

Introduction

About a century ago, Oscar Wilde posed the question of whether art reflected life or whether life reflected art. Much the same question could be asked about religion—do the gods reflect man or does man reflect the gods? For the Hindus, this conundrum might hardly even rate as an issue. For them, the gulf between the gods and men is not so distinct. They have a fabulous phantasmagoria of deities in their pantheon, a god for every occasion and contingency. In the Occident, however, our choice is somewhat limited, for the august figure of Jesus Christ dominates the occidental religious stage as the sun dominates the day. It can be granted that the stage he dominates is much smaller than it used to be as many of the more affluent parts of the Western world have become largely secularised. Apart from in the United States of America, the religious concerns of the churches in the wealthy countries of the West have, for the most part, been reduced to managing charitable concerns and the rituals surrounding births, deaths and marriages. It is the beauty of the cathedral, not its supposed significance, that is part of national heritage and attracts the tourists. But Jesus Christ is still the only fully scheduled and accredited Western god, many legal and parliamentary institutions pay lip service to him, and the anniversaries of his birth and death continue to constitute the bases of at least two annual holidays in many countries. His name is also a much favoured curse word. In short, he is our ancestral deity (I speak as an Australian).

But why? How did this come about, and what was it about Jesus himself that allowed him to gain so much status? The ancient world was polytheistic, and all cities and cultures had their own flourishing tutelary deities and divinities, most of whom have long since been relegated to the old gods' home. How did this particular deity manage to push them all aside and then go on to maintain his monopoly for the best part of two thousand years?

The Age of Reason dealt him a serious blow. There was a time when our ancestors attributed everything they could not understand to the machinations of the gods, so they prayed for sufficient rain and sunshine to make their crops grow. In medieval times, Christians prayed to Jesus for much the same things. When the broad base of Western society was agrarian, it was only natural that what men and women most desired from providence was good weather and healthy children—and plenty of them too, to replace those that will die in the next war. It was left to the king to handle affairs of state. In such a static social environment, Jesus' dominance of the celestial realms went largely unchallenged.

In a more scientific age, however, it is proving increasingly difficult for Jesus to hold his own, if only for the reason that he has become irrelevant to so many exigencies of modern living. Would one consult a bible when seeking to understand a computer program, for example? Can we seriously imagine the residents of a suburb where a nuclear facility was being installed feeling secure that there were no safety problems to worry about because the technicians who built it had prayed for it to function properly? Our not too distant ancestors did not have to suspend their rational faculties in order to maintain their religious beliefs, but we can no longer claim this privilege. The resurgence of strident American Christian fundamentalism, and the comical attempts to make Jesus sound "cool", may be the last gasps of a dying religion, the death rattle of a disappearing deity. To hear the virtues of Jesus being promoted to the beat of rap music would make the founding fathers of Christianity roll in their graves. However, tradition will ensure that Jesus maintains his heavenly occupancy—if not his monopoly—for some time, but, barring a major collapse of Western civilisation, the march of science and technology will ultimately spell his demise. As he has enjoyed such a long reign, it is appropriate we ask what events transpired to afford him his enormous success.

"Et Tu, Judas?—*Then Fall Jesus!*" propounds that there is a solid historical reason why Jesus conquered the old gods and secured an exclusive franchise on the Western heavens. But things are not always what they seem, and it will be argued that the origin of Christianity has nothing to do with the qualities, attributes or fortunes of a man called Jesus of Nazareth. Moreover, the explanation for its success is to be found in an entirely different, and much larger, arena than is commonly supposed. Chaos theory is not an attempt to prove that the flap of a butterfly wing can cause a cyclone, but is rather concerned with issues of predictability in complex systems. Minor events can occasion great outcomes, but great events are much more likely to.

In itself, the deification of Jesus presents a peculiar irony. According to the gospels, he was supposed to be the Jewish Messiah, a man with an enormous popular following with pretensions to being the King of the Jews. Just at the point when this seemed to be about to come to pass, he was treacherously betrayed and executed. However, rather than becoming the king of the Jews as he was touted to be, he in fact ultimately became the official god of the Roman Empire—the very power that destroyed the nation he was seeking regnancy over.

For those who are not familiar with the Jesus drama, we should look at a thumbnail sketch of the significant events in his career as depicted in our gospels. Around the age of thirty years, and in approximately 30 AD by our reckoning, Jesus suddenly appears on the scene and presents himself before a man known as John the Baptist on the banks of the river Jordan in Palestine, and is promptly baptized by him. John, himself a figure of no mean status, immediately recognizes Jesus as his spiritual superior. A voice from the heavens, presumed to be that of the Hebrew ancestral deity, declares that Jesus is his son, and that he is pleased with him (for reasons which are not stated).

Shortly afterwards, Jesus heads into the wilds, where Satan endeavours to tempt him into worshipping him, which Jesus steadfastly refuses to do. Satan soon realises his efforts are futile, and desists and decamps. On leaving the wilderness, Jesus collects twelve men to himself as his disciples, apparently by sheer force of charisma. He then embarks on a Blitzkrieg career of teaching, faith healing and magic, trekking from village to village in Galilee with his now faithful troop. He strides into synagogues and astounds the parishioners with his audacious preaching, but more particularly with the miracles he performs. Now he has a problem because huge crowds follow him everywhere he goes, and he becomes so popular that he has to resort to subterfuge to avoid them, even if just to get some sleep.

Increasingly he raises the ire of the established civil and religious authorities, usually described generically as "the scribes and Pharisees". He reciprocates their ill will by referring to them in unabashedly hostile terms, warning his followers to beware of them, and tagging them with such epithets as "spawn of Satan" or "generation of vipers". The scribes and Pharisees take exception to this, and plot to silence him once and for all. However, this is difficult to accomplish because he is constantly accompanied by adoring and hailing crowds.

At an indefinite point, Simon Peter, his chief disciple, declares that Jesus is the Son of God; Jesus affirms this to be true and appoints Peter as his right-hand man and first priest. From then on, Jesus starts telling his disciples that he has to go to Jerusalem to be arrested and executed, after which he will return from the dead. It is not clear whether any of them either understand or believe this, even though Jesus repeatedly tells them that it must happen. He finally seizes the moment, saddles up a donkey and rides triumphantly into the Holy City of Jerusalem, hailed as king by masses along a way strewn with palm fronds. He storms into the sacred temple brandishing a whip and drives out the moneychangers and merchants purveying sacrificial animals to the pious. He engages in a number of disputes with the Pharisees, all engendering their antagonism. The religious hierarchy become set on killing him—apparently for his reformist views and regal pretensions—but they still have the problem of apprehending him when he's unprotected by hordes of admirers.

Their big chance arrives unexpectedly, a day or so before the celebration of the feast of the Passover. Out of the blue, Judas Iscariot, one of Jesus' disciples, offers to deliver Jesus to them in secret. Overjoyed, they seize the option and even give him some money. Late on the Passover evening, Judas leads a troop of temple police to where Jesus is, and he is brought before a religious tribunal. There he is accused and found guilty of blasphemy. The very next morning the priests deliver him to the Roman governor, Pontius Pilate, where it would appear that Jesus is sentenced to death, by popular demand, for claiming to be the King of the Jews. For this he is duly crucified, and the moment of the occasion is captured in a portentous speech that Jesus delivers to a group of women as he walks the last mile to a place with the ominous name of Golgotha—

> *Weep not for me, O daughters of Jerusalem*
> *But for yourselves, and for your children.*
> *For the day is coming when they shall say*
> *Blessed are the barren,*
> *The wombs that never bore,*
> *And the paps that never gave suck.*
> *For then they shall say to the mountains, Fall on us*
> *And to the Hills, cover us.*
> *For if they do these things in the green tree*
> *What shall they do in the dry?*

But a few days after his execution, he rises from the dead, much to the rapture and surprise of even his most immediate supporters, who are then instructed to go out and spread the glorious news of his resurrection and "the kingdom of God". In the Christian scheme of things, this is the greatest moment in history, and the foundation event of Christianity itself.

But is it historical? The romantic view is that the religion started amongst a group of poor fishermen and nobodies whose zeal and preparedness for martyrdom ultimately conquered a hostile and unbelieving world. In the face of persecution, they dauntlessly went forth and preached the "gospel of Jesus Christ", being mercilessly thrown into the maws of hungry lions for their faith. And that the source for all this enthusiasm was the magnetic personality and teachings of Jesus himself, who arose triumphant from the tomb almost two millennia ago—

> *O Death, where is thy sting?*
> *O Grave, where is thy victory?*

The principal sources for the Jesus story are the four gospels in the New Testament, and it is commonly believed that the accounts related there must, perhaps minus a miracle or two, more or less accord with historical truth. More precisely, it is thought that there must have been a real flesh and blood man called Jesus who had a massive impact on those that met him, and this man must have been crucified. This is what we might call the minimalist Jesus theory. The theory presented in this book, however, is that these are not the events which gave birth to Christianity, and that the execution of a Jesus of Nazareth—if it occurred at all—simply would not have been important enough to start a religion that grew to be as great as Christianity. Evidence will be adduced to demonstrate that the earliest Christian churches knew nothing about the Jesus that most people today associate with Christianity, and that the churches were extant long before the gospels were written.

Far from giving us a comprehensive account of Jesus' life and the history of Christianity, it will be argued that the New Testament actually conceals more than it reveals, as much of it was written by men more interested in propaganda than facts. When looking into the origins of a religion, it is important to ascertain whether certain things were actually believed. Traditional religions, passed on culturally, tend to blind the recipients to the nature of what it is they think they believe in. The very word "belief" implies lack of ratiocination. Modern Christians, for example, would regard a practice like human sacrifice as something that belongs to man's dark and barbaric past. Yet Christian theology features a positive interpretation of just such a human sacrifice—that of Jesus Christ—and proudly expresses its central theme in atavistically sacrificial and expiatory terms. The Christian might object that the sacrifice of Jesus has special significance, and that can be granted—it may have special meaning for the Christian. But human sacrifice had special meaning to the Aztecs as well. The priest who tore your heart out was probably otherwise a very good neighbour.

So turning to Christianity, we must look to the oldest record we have of the circumstances of the death of Christ. It is generally agreed today that the gospel of "Mark" is the most ancient of the four housed within the New Testament, although it came to be positioned in second place after Matthew in the canon.

There is no apocryphal gospel held to be of earlier birth. Both the authors of "Matthew" and "Luke" had Mark's work open in front of them when they wrote their versions, a fact easily established by comparing the texts. Matthew incorporates about 90% of Mark, and Luke retains over 50%.

Matthew and Luke have other material in common that does not appear in Mark. German bible critics have posited the existence of a "Q" document—from *Quelle* meaning source—to which they must have had access. This seems to have consisted mostly of teachings and parables, but little biographical material, for when the two authors resort to it, the material they commonly employ appears in different points of time and circumstances in their accounts of Jesus' life borrowed from Mark. Due to this fact, and also on the basis of serious contradictions in their gospels, it can be deduced that Matthew and Luke were probably unaware of each other's writing.

Because of their general similarities, the gospels of Mark, Matthew and Luke are referred to as *synoptic*, meaning "viewed together". The latest of the canonised gospels, that of John, cannot be read in tandem with any of the others until one gets to the account of Jesus' "Passion". When constructing this gospel, the author decided to throw any attempt to accord with the synoptics to the winds, as his principal concern was to portray Jesus as a kind of incarnated beam of light surrounded by uncomprehending and hostile darkness. That he chose not to tamper too radically with the Passion material at the end of his gospel is a good indication of its status at the time of writing.

All of this is very important because the original gospel, Mark's, is very brief and can be read in an hour or so. Mark purports that Jesus had a substantial career, but gives us very little detail of what it consisted. Taken as read, it has been calculated that if Jesus' forty-day stint in the desert is excluded, the whole of his described activities could be wrapped up in about three weeks. The life of Jesus is truncated and rapid fire; there is little in the way of two-way conversation until the Passion story where there are large segments that appear to represent real time. In fact the Passion piece comprises about 40% of Mark's gospel, which has accordingly been dubbed "a Passion with a preface" or "a Passion with an extended introduction". Even today, Christianity emphasises this aspect of Jesus' career more than any other, as its salvation theology is based on the meaning and significance of his death.

The trial and execution of Jesus is commonly held to be a great historical injustice perpetrated against a good man. For this reason the present work begins with a brief look at some difficulties in the Passion accounts, starting with and mostly concentrating on Mark's, and then offers some thoughts on how they might have arisen.

Problems with Passion Week

Forgive me, Dionysius, I did not know

In the fourteenth chapter of Mark's story, we read that two days before an unspecified Passover in Jerusalem, the chief priests and scribes want to seize Jesus and kill him, but they sensibly agree—

> "Not on the feast day, lest it cause an uproar amongst the people." (Mk 14:1–2)

All very well, Jesus is portrayed as being popular and surrounded by admirers and supporters, so it would not be wise to apprehend him on an occasion as solemn and sacred as the Passover, which is what is meant by "the feast day." Perhaps on the same day, we find Jesus and his twelve disciples at the house of a chap called "Simon the Leper" in a place called Bethany, dining. A woman pours expensive oil over Jesus' head, which causes "some" of those present to ask themselves why this costly oil should not have been sold and the proceeds thereof distributed to the indigent.

Jesus upbraids them for their grumbling, and tells them that he won't always be with them, but that "the poor" are a permanent fixture. Besides, the woman is anointing him for burial, therefore it is a worthwhile investment. Slightly later, on the eve of the Passover, we find Jesus and "the twelve" in a pre-arranged guesthouse where they are alone in an upper room, feasting. Mark makes little effort to describe the general mood in the room at this point, but Jesus must have caused some consternation when he abruptly blurted out—

> "Verily, I say unto you, one of you which eateth with me shall betray me." (v 18)

Disconcerted, the disciples ask one by one—"Is it I?" Giving little away, Jesus says—

> "It is one of the twelve, that dippeth with me in the dish."

He then tempers what sounds like a remarkably casual attitude on his part with a declamation—

> "The Son of man indeed goeth, but woe unto that man by whom the Son of man is betrayed! Good were it for that man if he had never been born." (v 21)

These twelve men have been sharing Jesus' life and thoughts for some time and are supposedly all comrades. We might expect this terrible threat to induce them to stop eating and, hopefully, make some effort to ascertain who the betrayer is and take some preventive action. But apparently not—they just continue dining. Jesus stands up and distributes bread and wine to everyone present (presumably including the prospective betrayer). He then says—

> "Verily I say unto you, I will drink no more of the fruit of the vine until that day when I drink it anew in the Kingdom of God." (v 25)

Even this remarkable statement seems to elicit little curiosity. They all just sing a hymn, and then adjourn to the Mount of Olives. Here, Jesus tells his clique that, because it is written, they will all desert him that night; but when he is risen from the dead, he will go before them into Galilee. This news does upset the chief disciple Peter, who declares that even if all the others abandon Jesus, he won't. Jesus then avers that before the chook crows twice, he—Peter—will thrice deny knowing him. Peter vehemently declares that even if it were to mean his own death, he would never do such a thing. All the others express similar sentiments.

The troop then shifts to a garden called Gethsemane, and Jesus tells them to sit down while he goes aside to pray. He takes Peter, James and John with him, expresses his sadness, and tells them to keep watch. Unfortunately, it is not made clear what they are supposed to watch for. Jesus advances farther into the garden and then throws himself headlong to the ground and prays to his "father" to let the hour of tribulation pass him by, but then says—

> "Nevertheless, not what I will, but what thou wilt." (v 36)

He returns to find the three asleep, and chides them for not staying awake and watching. This time he tells them to watch and pray, lest they enter into temptation, but again it is not clear what the temptation might be. He goes away again, repeats his prayer, and comes back to find them asleep once more—to their embarrassment. Now he must have gone away a *third* time because he comes back again and finds them asleep yet again, and says—

> "Sleep on now, and take your rest; it is enough, the hour is come; behold, the Son of man is betrayed into the hands of sinners. Rise up, let us go; Lo, he that betrayeth me is at hand."
> (vs 41-2)

It would be nice to be able to ask Mark who witnessed Jesus' words if these three men were asleep. He does not tell us that Jesus woke them up before he spoke these words, so he must have been talking to himself, as it would seem unlikely that he would wake them up to tell them to go back to sleep only to tell them to wake up again in the very next sentence. The apparent tone of resignation in the words attributed to him suggests that his men were supposed to have been watching out for the arresting posse. This implies that if it were possible, he wanted to avoid being taken into custody. Had this happened, of course, it would have rendered his repeated predictions for the coming night incorrect. But the only way to make sense of his apparent frustration is to infer that his men let him down. In any event, it was too late. For even as he was still speaking, Judas—described as "one of the twelve"—arrived, accompanied by—

> "A great multitude with swords and staves, from the chief priests, the scribes and the elders." (v 43)

We must presume at this point that the other eight disciples left behind in the forward echelon of defence had also been sleeping, otherwise Judas' disappearance should have made them suspicious in light of the fact that Jesus had told them that one of them would betray him. Somehow, Mark must have found out that Judas had arranged a sign for the police to identify Jesus, as he provides us with the actual words that Judas said to them—

> "Whomsoever I shall kiss, the same is he; take him, and lead him away safely." (v 44)

Judas must have been confident that Jesus wouldn't pull away from him. He steps forward, kisses Jesus and says "Master, Master." The priestly deputation then seizes Jesus, and "one of them that stood by" lops an ear off one of the High

Priest's servants. Oddly, no attempt is made to detain this man. Jesus then rounds on the arresting squad—

> "Are ye come out, as against a thief, with swords and with staves
> to take me? *I was daily with you in the temple preaching*, and ye
> took me not—but the scripture must be fulfilled." (v 49)

This quote presents a multitude of problems. We can probably dismiss the claim that Jesus said "but the scripture must be fulfilled", as it would render his own complaint meaningless. But his question about why they had come out against him with swords and staves is easily answered by Mark himself, who told us earlier that Jesus had recently stormed into the above-mentioned temple, smashed property, assaulted people and driven them out of there by force (Mk 11:15). Consonant with this, one of his supporters had just sliced one of the official posse's ears off, so they must have been armed themselves. But the big problem with Jesus' complaint about being daily with these men in the temple is that it renders Judas' identifying kiss superfluous, as the obvious implication is that many of these men knew Jesus by sight. If Jesus were aware that many of the arresting posse already knew him, a more pertinent question for him to ask would be "Why did Judas have to kiss me?" The narrative continues—

> "And they all forsook him, and fled." (v 50)

This "all" presumably means all his disciples except Judas, and it's probably safe to infer that they fled for fear of arrest. But now a curious incident—

> "And there followed him (Jesus) a certain young man, having a
> linen cloth cast about his naked body, and the young men laid
> hold on him: And he left the linen cloth, and fled from them
> naked." (vs 51-2)

Now who was he? This "naked youth" reference has caused an enormous amount of speculation, particularly revolving around the question of why such an apparently petty detail should have been inserted into what purports to be a very serious narrative. Rather than enter this controversy, we'll just deal with the information as it stands. Mark already told us that the arresting party consisted of a "great multitude" with swords and staves. The fact that they tried to seize this "young man" would suggest that they took him to be a follower or supporter of Jesus. Why, then, did not at least some of this "great multitude" pursue him? And if they wanted to apprehend him because he was a follower of Jesus, why was no attempt made to pursue the other, far more important, disciples? Bear in mind that one of them just committed a savage assault with a weapon.

After this, Jesus is led to the High Priest's palace, where the Sanhedrin, the council of the priests, elders and scribes are assembled. Peter has followed at a distance, and is now, amazingly enough, in the palace grounds, warming himself by a fire with the house servants. This is another indication that the priestly deputation didn't have much interest in detaining any of the disciples; they could at least have left a rear guard in case any of the disciples followed them. (It should be noted in passing that the night was cold enough for the servants to be sitting around a fire, which further highlights the curiousness of the episode of the scantily clad lad.) Inside the High Priest's palace, Mark tells us that many "false witnesses" were borne against Jesus, but unfortunately he only details one of them—

> "And there arose certain…saying, 'We heard him say, I will destroy this temple made with hands, and within three days I will build another made without hands.'" (v 58)

Mark doesn't tell us anywhere in his gospel that Jesus said these words (other gospels do!), so we will take his word that it was a false witness. He goes on to inform us that "neither so did their witness agree together", but fails to provide us with any examples of contradictory accusations. The matter of how Mark might have found out what words were exchanged inside the palace is also pertinent, but will be dealt with later. The High Priest, Caiaphas (name construed from Mt and Jn), then asks Jesus to respond to the various allegations, but receives no answer. Presumably frustrated, he comes straight out with—

> "Art thou the Christ, the Son of the Blessed?" (v 61)

—perhaps giving him the cue to let himself off the hook, but Jesus responds with—

> "I am—and ye shall see the Son of man sitting on the right hand of power, and coming in the clouds of heaven." (v 62)

—whereupon the High Priest rends his coat in mortification at the "blasphemy". Jesus is then spat upon, buffeted and mocked by some of those present—including the servants! Meanwhile, downstairs and presumably in the forecourt, Peter has been recognised by one of the maids. She says—

> "And thou also was with Jesus of Nazareth!" (v 67)

The maid might have been zealous of religious matters, but where did she meet Peter? A lowly maid recognizes Jesus' sidekick but a multitudinous *posse comitatus* needed Judas' signifying kiss to identify the leader Jesus out of a maximum line-up of only eleven. Peter somewhat over-reacts to the maid's allegation—

> "I know not, neither understand I what thou sayest." (v 68)

He moves out onto the porch and "the cock crew". Now *another* maid sees him, and begins to say to those standing around "This is one of them"—which strongly implies that all of Jesus' disciples were wanted men and again raises the question of why the arresting band did not pursue them when they fled. Following this second denial by Peter, the heat seems to ease off for a while, until—

> "…a little later, they that stood by said again to Peter, 'surely thou art one of them—for thou art a Galilean, and thy speech agreeth thereto.' But he began to curse and to swear, saying, 'I know not this man of whom ye speak.'" (vs 70-1)

Now the chook crows a second time, and Peter belatedly recalls Jesus' prediction and bursts into tears. As far as Mark is concerned, this is the end of this particular episode, as the very next paragraph presents a change in time and place. But before we leave it ourselves, we must ask why these people were accusing Peter of being "one of them". It seems they were content when he started crying not to pursue the matter any further—they had no intention of taking action against him, they only wanted to know if he knew Jesus out of idle curiosity.

However, if there were no menace in the manner in which these people were asking him if he knew Jesus, then his denial of knowing him would seem to have little significance. To give the denial pathos, Peter would have needed to feel himself under some threat—the most obvious being that of arrest with worse things to follow. Had Peter broken down and wept on the spot (as we are told), it would have been fairly clear indication that he was lying, and presumably he would have been arrested. If he simply walked away without crying, surely his interrogators would have apprehended him for further questioning. And of course, had he *run* away, there would have been all the more reason for pursuing him. So whichever course he chose, how is it that no further action was taken? The curious must remain frustrated, for the next verse transports us to the morning of the first day of unleavened bread. The chief priests consult and then hurriedly bustle Jesus off to front the Roman governor, Pontius Pilate, whose first question to Jesus is—

"Art thou the king of the Jews?" (Mk 15:2)

When Jesus had earlier responded affirmatively to the question of whether he was the "Son of the Blessed", the Sanhedrin had considered him worthy of death for the crime of blasphemy under Jewish religious law. However, the issue before Pilate is rather political and concerns Roman law—self-proclaimed kings were a threat to the existing Roman appointed Jewish kings and by extension the then emperor Tiberius Caesar. Jesus responds to Pilate's question with an ambiguous "Thou sayest"(Mk 15:2). Mark again reports that the chief priests accused Jesus of many things, but again doesn't specify what they were. Pilate asks Jesus to answer the charges, which he curiously refuses to do. It is worth noting that this trial is held by most Christians to be a historical event and a pathetic travesty of justice. Perjury is universally regarded as inimical to the rule of law. The fact that Mark does not specify what the false charges laid against Jesus were gives rise to the suspicion that he is trying to heighten the perfidy of the "trial" by having the accusers blatantly and repeatedly break the ninth Mosaic commandment—

"Thou shalt not bear false witness against thy neighbour." (Ex 20:16)

However, in not identifying the nature of the false accusations, the gospel writer himself is making unsubstantiated allegations. Mark could hardly know the allegations were false unless he knew precisely what they were. He further tells us that Jesus made no attempt to answer the charges. Where did Mark get the information about what transpired during the earlier Sanhedrin inquest? We can rule out the possibility that the priests themselves told him. Imagine them saying to Mark, obviously a supporter of Jesus, "…well, you see Mark, we falsely accused him of many things." It is frustrating, to say the least, that he failed to tell us what these allegations were and how he found out about them. It leaves us with no means of establishing the rights and wrongs of the case.

He proceeds to tell us that Pilate had a custom (which no one seems able to trace) of releasing a prisoner during the feast of the Passover, and that the "multitude" cried aloud to Pilate demanding that he do so on this occasion. Pilate asks them if they want him to release the "King of the Jews"—

"For he perceived that it was out of envy that the chief priests had delivered him (Jesus) up." (Mk 15:10)

Mark now relates that the chief priests somehow stirred up "the people" to demand the release of a different prisoner instead—a man who in the oldest codices that the church father Origen could find was named "Jesus Barabbas" (Jesus son of the father!) That the priests should have wanted to release Barabbas is disturbing, as Mark tells us that Barabbas had "committed murder in the insurrection" (15:7). We can infer that the insurrection was recent, and that his victim (or victims) must have been Roman or a person (or persons) in cahoots with them. Hopefully we can write off the possibility that the chief priests would really have wanted to kill Jesus if they believed him to be the son of God, so we have to look for another motive. There is the eternal possibility of plain old jealousy, as Mark alleges, but a more likely one is that Jesus was seen as a threat to the delicate Jewish/Roman relationship in that he might have had the potential to cause an uprising. This is the real reason the 1st century Jewish historian Josephus furnishes us with for why Herod Antipas executed John the Baptist (see *AJ*, XVIII, 109–116). The priests would have in mind that the resultant Roman backlash would mean great slaughter for their own people, or even worse.

A released Barabbas, then, could do the same thing—particularly as he reportedly had already been involved in at least one political killing! Mark later tells us (15:27) that Jesus was crucified between two thieves, so why didn't the priests stir up the crowds to release one of these lesser threats to the status quo than Barabbas was? Their reported action would appear to have been against the interests of both themselves and the Romans. If we take the story as read, we have to believe that Pilate was perspicacious enough to realise that the chief priests delivered Jesus to him out of envy, but apparently not enough to notice that they stirred the crowd up against Jesus, for after the crowd demand that Barabbas be released, Pilate asks them—

> "What will ye then that I shall do unto him whom ye call the
> King of the Jews?" (Mk 15:12)

If they really had, just a few days earlier, hailed Jesus as their king, which by implication Pilate confirms, would they have responded to his question as Mark tells us they did—

> "Crucify him!" (v 13)?

Why would these people have so suddenly turned against Jesus? The chief priests could hardly have incited the crowds by telling them that Jesus said he was the Messiah if they already believed he was. And they could not have stirred them up by telling them that Jesus was claiming to be the king of the Jews if they were the ones who had hailed him as such. So how did the chief priests achieve this? Some have suggested that the people turned hostile towards Jesus because they had been hoping that he would set up a temporal kingdom of God, and then all of a sudden they saw him arrested. They were disillusioned to such an extent that they actively turned against him and called loudly for his death. Going along with this theory, we must ask how those people envisioned that Jesus would set up his kingdom. If the powers-that-were had refused to go along with Jesus' plan, he possibly could have used supernatural force to get his way. But if the people believed him capable of that, they certainly took an enormous risk by calling for his death. How would they have known that Jesus wasn't just "playing it cool", allowing himself to be arrested to provide a dramatic touch when he suddenly burst forth from his bonds into supernatural glory? Surely such a crowd should have feared that Jesus might just take careful note of those demanding his crucifixion and then zap them all in a blinding flash! In short, no one would call for the death of someone they regarded as a supernatural being.

On the other hand, if they *did not* believe that he had preternatural powers but wanted him as their king, then the only way he could have set up his Kingdom would have been by employing his charisma to rouse a following, call for a democratic election or utilise brute force to achieve his ends. If they had thought he would use *this* means, then seeing him arrested should have incited his multitudinous supporters to rebellion. Now was the very time to take action.

In an apparent effort to save him, Pilate demands of the crowd to know what evil Jesus has done (has the poor man forgotten the priests' accusations already?), but—

> "…they cried out all the more exceedingly, Crucify him! And so Pilate, *willing to content the people*, released Barabbas unto them, and delivered Jesus, when he had scourged him, to be crucified." (Mk 15:15)

The soldiers lead Jesus away, and—

> "…they clothed him with purple, and platted a crown of thorns, and put it on him. And they began to salute him, Hail king of the Jews!" (Mk 15:17-8)

Note that Jesus is here being savaged for his royal pretensions. They spit on him and beat him, and pay mock homage to him in his regal attire, then lead him away this time to be crucified—

"…and it was the third hour when they crucified him." (v 25)

So the crucifixion began about nine o'clock in the morning by our reckoning. Again there are problems here. Mark told us earlier that the chief priests didn't want to seize Jesus on the feast day as it might cause a "tumult" among the people, so they took him at night, in secret. If Jesus really had a popular following, this was a reasonably smart thing to do. But the next day, the first day of the holy festival, they trundle Jesus on down to Pilate and incite "the crowd" to pressure Pilate to crucify him—*post haste*! The city would have been full of pilgrims from out of town; estimates of attendance at the Jerusalem Passover in those days vary from 50,000 to 200,000 (probably closer to the former). So there would have been huge numbers of them, and Mark claims that the chief priests got their way and had Jesus openly displayed on the cross by nine in the morning.

How would "the people" know what had taken place during the night? Would not at least half of the people considered likely to cause a tumult wonder what Jesus was doing up there on the cross, and (a) be angry about it and (b) make urgent enquiries as to how it came about? And if they found out that the chief priests had used these underhand measures to nab Jesus, would they not have been even the more incensed? Mark tells us that Jesus' fame had spread throughout the back blocks, huge crowds waited on his miracles as he dispensed food to thousands, healed the sick, bedazzled them with revolutionary preaching and cast out demons. These country folk are now streaming through the streets of Jerusalem, when lo and behold they find out that this beloved preacher and miracle-worker has been strung up on a cross. Not only that, but on this holy day as well!

But we are told that a "multitude" screamed out for Jesus' death, leaving the beleaguered Pilate with no choice but to capitulate. Who were they, and what happened to Jesus supporters? The famous movie scenes where we see Jesus' loyal followers being drowned out or pushed back by the howling mob are apologetic; they are not supported by the gospel authors who make scant effort to explain the turnabout. Mark says of Jesus making his triumphal entry into Jerusalem just a few days earlier—

> "And many spread their garments on the road, and others spread leafy branches which they had cut from the fields. And those that went before and those that followed cried out: Hosanna! Hosanna! Blessed is he who comes in the name of the Lord! Blessed is the Kingdom of our father David that is coming! Hosanna in the highest!" (Mk 11:8–10)

So Jesus was ushered into the city with an advance and rear guard of cheering supporters. Where were they when he needed them most? And what happened to his disciples? So what if those dodgy chief priests had abandoned their wonted decorum and stirred up a few rabble-rousers outside the Praetorium? Jesus' disciples should have been crying blue murder in the streets, banging on doors and storming the synagogues to rally support for their master. And Mark tells us that when Jesus was being crucified he was still alive at the ninth hour (15:34). That's six full hours from the time when Jesus was first publicly displayed on the cross—plenty of time to get an eleventh hour "letter from the governor", indeed a governor who had already shown his willingness to save Jesus.

The chief priests had risked a major insurrection totally unnecessarily. If they really had wanted to get Jesus out of the way after they had arrested him that night, would it not have been easier to just let him "fall down the stairs"? Or, if they still wanted to have him tried, why didn't they just get Pilate to hold him over for a while, at least until the Passover week had finished and the country pilgrims—the principle beneficiaries of his miracles and teachings—had left the city and returned to their farms and flocks?

Mark and the other three gospel writers portray the chief priests as incorrigibly evil, but we also have to believe them rather stupid as well. If we accept that they were hell-bent on killing Jesus, then they took a major risk in bringing him to Pilate—especially if they were familiar with his practice of releasing a prisoner on Passover, as they would have been if the custom existed. They could have lost their opportunity to dispose of him. Had Jesus been merely found slumped in a back lane, an itinerant beggar or a hoodlum could easily have been blamed or framed for the crime. But if Jesus were found the victim of foul play after an unsuccessful bid by the chief priests to have him executed, obviously they would be the prime suspects.

There is nothing in our records of Pilate to suggest that he would have acted with the sense of reasonableness we read of in the gospels. We know from Josephus that Pilate had once appropriated money from the Jerusalem temple to improve the city's water supply, causing an insurrection. He dressed Roman soldiers as civilians and had them infiltrate the protesting crowd. At a given signal, they produced concealed daggers and set upon the demonstrators, killing and wounding large numbers. In another incident Pilate had tried to introduce standards bearing the image of Tiberius Caesar, over the objections of the pious, into Jerusalem overnight. Again he had Roman soldiers surround the Jewish protesters, who threw themselves to the ground *en masse* and bared their necks to the sword. It was only when Pilate pondered how he would justify to Tiberius the large numbers he would need to slaughter that he relented (see *BJ*, II, 169–177). The Jewish historian Philo of Alexandria described Pilate as merciless and obstinate, and he ultimately had to be recalled to Rome after he slaughtered a band of Samaritans who had been persuaded by a prophet that he knew the location of certain sacred vessels hidden by Moses. This is strong evidence of Pilate's callousness, as Tiberius was status quo oriented and renowned for recalling his administrators only when it was absolutely necessary. In short, Pilate does not sound like the kind of man who would meekly bow to the will of the chief priests as he does in the gospels. Even if we assume Pilate to have been a sensitive soul, the gospel descriptions of his actions are still difficult to understand. The Jesus trial was not something he initiated, so his best course of action would have been to hold Jesus over—"make him sweat"—at least long enough to investigate the facts and determine whether it was in his own interests to prosecute the case or not. But by no means would he be forced to execute Jesus *contre-coeur*.

Coming back to Mark's story, he tells us that when Jesus was crucified the superscription "King of the Jews" was attached to his cross. Then we read—

> "And they that passed by railed on him, wagging their heads, and saying, Ah, thou that destroyeth the temple, and buildest it in three days, save thyself, and come down from the cross. Likewise also the chief priests mocking said among themselves with the scribes, He saved others; himself he cannot save. Let Christ the king of Israel descend now from the cross, that we may see and believe. And they that were crucified with him reviled him. (Mk 15:29–32)

Who were the people passing by? They can't be the chief priests and scribes, as they are mentioned separately. We were told earlier that it had been a false witness that Jesus had said something about destroying and rebuilding the temple (14:58). The chief priests themselves must have spread the spurious story, and the gullible had believed it to the point of being prepared to pour scorn on Jesus for having said it—even the two thieves get in on the act! Also note that the chief priests and scribes refer to Jesus having saved people. This is not the salvation of standard Christian theology, as Jesus hasn't died at this point to provide the atoning sacrifice, so the saving must indicate such feats as Jesus raising Jairus' daughter from a narcosis (Mk 5:39–42) or his many exorcisms. We can hopefully surmise that the priests did not believe these miracles ever actually occurred, as it would seem unlikely that they would want to do away with a holy man of such prodigious and useful abilities.

From here on the story becomes magical, so we shall only look at it briefly. While Jesus is crucified, the sky darkens from midday till three o'clock in the afternoon. Shortly after this, Jesus breathes his last and yields up the ghost. Amongst the spectators watching his execution from a distance were Mary Magdalene, Mary the mother of "James the Less", and a certain Salome. Apparently they had all come up to Jerusalem with Jesus as part of his retinue. After he dies, Joseph of Arimathea—a man of reputed status and a friend of his, goes to Pilate and requests his body. Pilate "marvelled" that Jesus should have died so quickly, and after certifying that it is true, turns the body over to Joseph. He lays it in a tomb hewn in the side of a rock face and rolls a stone across the entrance. This burial takes place late on a Friday afternoon, as the next day is described as the Sabbath.

At sunrise the following Sunday, the two Marys and Salome arrive at the sepulchre and find that the stone has been rolled away from the entrance. They venture in and are taken aback by the sight of a young man in a long white garment who tells them not to be scared and that Jesus has risen. He then says—

> "But go your way, tell his disciples and Peter that he is going before you into Galilee; there you will see him, as he told you." (Mk 16:7)

Mark continues—

> "And they went out and fled from the tomb; for trembling and astonishment had come upon them; and they said nothing to anyone; for they were afraid."

This is where the earliest versions of Mark's gospel ended, at verse 8 chapter 16. The next section (called the "false ending") has been added, and is redundant and contradictory—

> "Now when he rose early on the first day of the week, he appeared first unto Mary Magdalene, from whom he had cast seven devils. And she went and told them that had been with him, as they mourned and wept. And they, when they had heard that he was alive, and had been seen of her, believed not." (Mk 16:9–11)

Jesus finally appears to the "eleven" disciples (presumably Judas has defected) when they are having dinner, and upbraids them for not believing that he had already been seen (this presupposes that Jesus knew they had been told about this). His scolding is very curious, because when he delivered his "Olivet prophecy", he reportedly warned these very same disciples to later beware of false Christs after his passing, specifically telling them—

> "And then if any man shall say to you, Lo, here is Christ; or, Lo, he is there; *believe him not!*" (Mk 13:21)

After the posthumous reprimand, Jesus says—

> "Go into all the world and preach the gospel to every creature. He that believeth and is baptised shall be saved; but he that believeth not shall be damned. And these signs shall follow them that believe—in my name they shall cast out devils; they shall speak with new tongues; they shall take up serpents; and if they drink any deadly thing, it will not hurt them; they shall lay hands on the sick, and they shall recover." (vs 15-8)

At that, he ascends into the heavens. Thus ends our first Christian gospel, possibly the oldest record we have of something touted as good news being accompanied by a threat of damnation for those who would not believe it. But the promises of magical powers for believers soon proved to be an embarrassment, as from early times verses 9–20 were substituted with the more sober—

> "So then the Lord Jesus, after he had spoken to them, was taken up into heaven, and sat down at the right hand of God. And they went forth and preached everywhere, while the Lord worked with them and confirmed the message by the signs that attended it. Amen." (vs 19–20)

This seems to be the essence of the story—Jesus of Nazareth, a wonder-worker, great man and Son of God, falls foul of the authorities who think he wants to be king, and he is brought undone when he is betrayed by his disciple Judas and abandoned by his followers. He then suffers a miscarriage of justice and an execution, after which he rises from the dead. Millions believe this story has a historical basis, even if they don't accept the miracles. All of this is promoted in the NT and by the later Christian church as fulfilment of prophecy, the working out of a divine predetermined plan. Now we need to investigate just to what extent Jesus was betrayed, and whether, as some have suggested, the story was merely construed from prophecy.

The Traitor

Many books and even movies have been produced dealing with the personal relationship between Jesus and Judas Iscariot. Mostly these works have been concerned with exactly what might have motivated Judas to "betray" Jesus. The popular line of what we might coin "mainstream occultism" is that as Jesus' career developed he became increasingly ethereal and spoke more and more of some intangible heavenly kingdom of God. Judas, earthy and rash, decided to deliver Jesus to his enemies in order to "force his hand" into using his supernatural powers or charisma or a combination of both to seize the reins of power and establish a temporal kingdom of God in Jerusalem.

Enticing though some find it, this theory is baseless. It might be interesting to discover that Judas plays absolutely no role in any of the gospel stories until about six sentences before he precipitately races off to the chief priests to betray Jesus. All the colourful character portrayals of Judas developed in recent times are based on a mere *two words* (master, master) he allegedly spoke in Mark's original gospel, and a further fifteen words in reported speech. None of these words indicate that he had any political plans whatsoever. He is merely listed as being "one of the twelve" disciples who, with the possible exception of Peter, are basically faceless men in the story. There is no ground in the gospels for the notion that he had any kind of "special relationship" with Jesus. Those already aware of this might choose to skip this chapter, but I would recommend others read on.

We've already looked at what Mark has to say about Judas. Matthew provides us with a little more information. After the woman anoints Jesus with the expensive oil, Matthew's Judas, unlike Mark's, actually asks the chief priests for money *before* he consents to betray Jesus—

> "And he said unto them, What will ye give me, and I will deliver him unto you? And they covenanted with him for thirty pieces of silver." (Mt 26:15)

Likewise, Matthew's Jesus, during the "Last Supper", announces that one of those present will betray him, and the disciples all start asking "Is it I?" This time Jesus elaborates by saying—

"It is he that dippeth his hand with me in the dish."

Then we read—

"Judas, which betrayed him, answered and said, Master, is it I?
And he said unto him, Thou hast said." (26:25)

It is not clear from the text whether any of the other disciples heard it, but now at least Judas knows that Jesus knows that he is the prospective betrayer. So what happens? Nothing in particular. They just continue eating, and as in Mark, Jesus distributes the bread and the wine. And, also as in Mark, we are not told if or when Judas parts company with the rest of the band, but he suddenly reappears in verse 47 in the garden of Gethsemane, introduced with the same words: "Judas, one of the twelve." Judas is so insignificant in the gospel story thus far that Mark and Matthew see it necessary to remind us that he is "one of the twelve". For his part, Jesus seems to have forgotten his own Last Supper conversation because he asks Judas—

"Friend, wherefore art thou come?" (Mt 26:50)

From here on events proceed pretty much as they did in Mark, except that Matthew adds a significant detail. Mark left us in the dark as to what happened to Judas after the betrayal, but Matthew makes no such oversight. After the chief priests deliver Jesus to Pilate, we read—

"Then Judas, which betrayed him, when he saw that he was condemned, repented himself, and brought again the thirty pieces of silver to the chief priests and elders, saying, I have sinned in that I have betrayed innocent blood. And they said, What is that to us? See thou to it. And he cast down the pieces of silver in the temple and departed, and went and hanged himself. And the chief priests took the silver pieces, and said, It is not lawful for to put them into the treasury, because it is the price of blood. And they took counsel, and bought with them the potter's field, to bury strangers in. Wherefore that field was called the field of blood, unto this day. Then was fulfilled that which was spoken by Jeremy the prophet, saying, And they

took the thirty pieces of silver, the price of him that was val-
ued, whom they of the children of Israel did value; and gave
them for the potter's field, as the Lord appointed me." (Mt
27:3–10)

Jeremy never really said this at all. However, he did write that "the Lord" had
told him that his cousin would ask him to buy a field at a place called Anathoth.
This happened as predicted, and Jeremy reports—

"And I bought the field at Anathoth from Hanamel my cousin,
and weighed out the money to him, even seventeen shekels of
silver." (Jeremiah 32:9)

The deal is then signed and sealed in the presence of the requisite authorities.
Jeremy tells his amanuensis Baruch—

"Thus saith the Lord of Hosts the God of Israel; Take these
evidences of the purchase, both which is sealed and that which
is open; and put them in an earthen vessel that they may continue many days. For thus saith the Lord of Hosts, the God of
Israel; Houses and fields and vineyards shall be possessed again
in this land." (Jer 32:14-5)

The symbolism of this appears to be that the Jews would return to their homeland after their captivity in Babylon. Now in the eighteenth and nineteenth chapters of Jeremiah, a potter's vessel is used as a symbol of the nation of Judah.
Because the people had "filled this place with innocent blood", the prophet is
instructed to buy a potter's vessel and smash it in the sight of the Jewish elders
and priests in a place called the "Potsherd Gate" to foreshadow the coming
destruction of the nation by Babylon. But all this really gives us is a tenuous link
between earthen vessels and silver pieces on the one hand, and a potter's vessel
and innocent blood on the other. It is a far cry from a prediction of the betrayal
of Jesus.

Matthew's reference to thirty pieces of silver actually comes from the book of
Zechariah, where the prophet likens himself to a sacrificial animal. After having
broken a staff called "Grace" that symbolises an end to God's caring for the flock
of Israel, he offers himself to the temple merchants—

"And I said unto them, If ye think good, give me my price; and
if not, forbear. So they weighed for my price *thirty pieces of silver*. And the Lord said unto me—Cast it unto the potter—a

goodly price that I was prised at of them. And I took the thirty pieces of silver and cast them to the potter in the house of the Lord. Then I cut asunder mine other staff, even Bands, that I might break the brotherhood between Judah and Israel." (Zech 11:12-4)

This "staff" was already well and truly broken by then. The "Israel" referred to above is the northern kingdom of Israel, the capital of which was Samaria. It had been conquered and taken captive by the Assyrians some 130 years before the Babylonians captured the southern kingdom of Judah. The name of this kingdom is traditionally derived from the name of one of the sons of the patriarch Israel, aka Jacob. Matthew has taken a historical reference to the splitting of the nations Judah and Israel, welded some discrete texts together, ascribed them to Jeremiah, and claimed them to be prophecies of Judas betraying Jesus. None of the other gospel writers refer to this. Matthew even changed Zechariah's "goodly" price of thirty pieces of silver for the land he bought into a bad price for Jesus.

But there *is* a precedent in Jewish tradition for the account of Judas hanging himself. Jeremiah had predicted a future resurrection or reincarnation of the ancient Israelite King David, after the yoke of captivity had been broken from the necks of Israel and Judah—

"They shall serve the Lord their God, and David their King, whom I shall raise up unto them." (Jer 30:9)

Matthew repeatedly identifies Jesus as the "son" of David (see e.g. Mt 1:6–16; 9:27; 12:23; 15:22; 20:30-1; 21:9, 15; 22:42). In terms of status in the Jewish hall of heroes, David ranks behind only Moses and the war leader Joshua (Jesus). We read in the Hebrew scriptures how a certain Ahithopel, after having counselled against or betrayed David—

"Set his house in order, and hanged himself." (2 Sam 17:23)

Of course, this "betrayal" of David didn't lead to his death. But this is probably where Matthew found his scriptural precedent, as Ahithopel still holds number one spot in the rabbinic hall of infamy. The authenticity of this description of Judas' demise is undermined by another version in the NT—

"And in those days Peter stood up in the midst of the disciples and said—"Men and brethren, this scripture must needs have been fulfilled, which the Holy Ghost by the mouth of David spake concerning Judas, which was guide to them that took

Jesus. For he was numbered with us and had obtained part of this ministry. Now this man purchased a field with the reward of iniquity; and falling headlong, he burst asunder in the midst, and all his bowels gushed out. And it was known unto all the dwellers in Jerusalem; insomuch as that field is called in their proper tongue 'Alceldama', that is to say, the Field of Blood." (Acts 1:15-9)

So it was called the Field of Blood because Judas bled there when his "bowels gushed out". But in Matthew's story it was dubbed the Field of Blood because the priests had bought it with the returned thirty pieces, the price of the "innocent blood" of Jesus. Also observe that Judas doesn't hang himself in this version. Notwithstanding this, the author of Acts, just like Matthew, claims that a prophecy was fulfilled—

"For it is written in the book of Psalms, Let his habitation be desolate, and let no man dwell therein." (v 20—part a)

The Book of Psalms does not really say this. The author of Acts has changed the text of Psalm 69 from the plural to the singular, for we read in the original—

"Let their habitation be desolate, and let none dwell in their tents. For they persecute him whom thou hast smitten, and they talk to the grief of those whom thou hast wounded. Add iniquity unto their iniquity, and let them not come into thy righteousness." (vs 25–27)

The Psalmist writes about people whom he refers to as "mine adversaries" (v 19), who were obviously giving him problems centuries before Judas could have existed. Referring to Judas, the author of Acts continues with his speech by having Peter quote scripture—

"And his bishopric let another take." (Acts 1:20, part b)

This text is taken from forty chapters later in the Book of Psalms, where the psalmist is beseeching God to curse his enemies, who are personified in the singular. Let me provide some context for the verse Acts has adapted—

"Let his days be few, and *let another take his office.* Let his children be fatherless, and his wife a widow. Let his children be continually vagabonds, and beg. Let them seek their bread also out of their desolate places." He finishes—"Let this be the reward of mine adversaries before the Lord, and of them that speak evil against my soul." (Ps 109:8–20)

So the Psalmist is calling general woe upon his adversaries in his own time, poetically alternating between the singular and the plural, but he is not predicting the betrayal of the Messiah several centuries later.

We now turn to Luke. This writer further demonises the character of Judas by omitting the story of the woman who wasted precious ointment by anointing Jesus' feet—the very event that was supposed to provoke the betrayal. If we compare Mark 14 with Luke 22, no other reasonable conclusion can be arrived at. In his 22nd chapter, Luke, copying from Mark, paraphrased the latter's first two verses with little change. Then he left out the next seven verses, and furnished his own reason why Judas had gone to the chief priests—

"Then entered Satan into Judas surnamed Iscariot, being of the number of the twelve." (Lk 22:3)

So Luke also helpfully reminds us that Judas is one of the twelve. After this, his account of events agrees with Mark's almost word for word. In promoting the good guy Jesus, let there be no mitigating circumstances for the behaviour of the villain. Luke's description of the response by the disciples to Jesus' announcement during the Last Supper that "The hand of the betrayer is with me on the table" is remarkable—

"And they began to enquire among themselves, which of them it was that should do this thing."

It might regale the human heart to learn they were alarmed that one of their number should betray their beloved Master, but they soon turned their attention to more pressing concerns—

"And there was also strife among them, which of them should be accounted the greatest." (22:24)

This weighty matter appears to have smothered the lesser issue of who the betrayer in their midst might be, and there is not even a hint that it occurred to any of these men to do something about it. As silly as this story sounds, it probably represents an attempt by Luke to patch up an awkward hole in Mark's account, *viz* why didn't the other disciples make a determined effort to find out just who the betrayer was and take some preventive action? Luke's answer? They were distracted by a controversy about which one of them was the holiest Joe!

But what about Jesus himself? It has been seriously suggested by some that Jesus might have planned his own execution at Passover so he could become a martyr and that he might have engineered that Judas betray him for his own noble or low reasons. If that were the case, then Jesus seriously risked not being betrayed and executed at all by letting all and sundry at the Supper know what was going to happen. Judas might well have broken down on the spot, confessing his intentions before the whole team. Jesus' cleverly timed Passover martyrdom would have been foiled.

Another variation of the "special relationship" theory is that Judas *conspired* with his master to have him executed in order to furnish a foundation martyr for the prospective religion (seriously). But this hypothesis also suffers from the same problem as before—why would Jesus risk the operation by spilling the beans in front of the other disciples? And more pertinently, why would Judas decide to kill himself when his mission had been so manifestly successful? A necessary concomitant of this popular theory is that the "special relationship" between the two players has been edited out of the NT because it did not suit the early church that people should think that Jesus and Judas were buddies. This is a case of absence of evidence being taken for presence of substance.

Luke, like Mark, does not tell us whether Judas slips away from the supper or not. "Judas, one of the twelve" just suddenly reappears in verse 47 where he steps forward to kiss Jesus, who utters the stinging words—

"Judas, betrayest thou the Son of Man with a kiss?" (v 47)

Jesus is then apprehended, and the text generally follows Mark. Judas now drops out of Luke's story, so we turn to John. This last of the canonised gospel authors has developed the theme of Judas' motive furthest. Rather than wait until the fatal Passover, John has Jesus being aware of the traitor much earlier. Unlike the version told by the synoptic authors, Jesus doesn't deliver the "Eucharist" at the Last Supper; in fact he and the twelve appear to have been eating for about two days before the infamous arrest. Jesus had made an earlier speech at a synagogue in the northern city of Capernaum, where he spoke of the need for his followers to eat his flesh and drink his blood. This sounded so distastefully literal that John says many of his acolytes walked off. Jesus then turns to the faithful "twelve", which obviously includes Judas, and asks them if they will do the same.

Speaking for the group, Peter assures Jesus that there is nowhere for them to go because Jesus alone has the key to eternal life. For no clear reason, Jesus says—

> "Have I not chosen you twelve, and one of you is a devil? He spoke of Judas Iscariot the son of Simon—for it was he that should betray him, being one of the twelve." (Jn 6:66–71)

One of the twelve again. As usual, frustration lies in ambush for the reader desirous of learning how Peter and the others responded to their master's disturbing question. The editor of John has placed this piece of dialogue right at the end of a chapter, the next opens in another place, leaving us in the dark as to what ensued. John's time sequences are difficult to ascertain, but many events occur between the incident at Capernaum and the ultimate betrayal. Jesus and his retinue travel around the countryside, he delivers sermons, argues with "the Jews" and raises Lazarus from the dead before turning up at a house in Bethany six days before the Passover. During all this time John does not record any controversy whatsoever amongst the disciples as to just who the "devil" in their midst might have been.

John repeats Mark's story of the events that took place in Bethany, but has the woman anointing Jesus' feet rather than his head. This time, however, it is *only Judas* who grumbles about the waste of expensive oil—

> "Then saith one of his disciples, Judas Iscariot, Simon's son, which should betray him, 'Why was not this ointment sold for three hundred pence and given to the poor?"

And just in case we might think Judas an altruist—

> "This he said, not that he cared for the poor; but because he was a thief, and had the bag, and bare what was put therein." (Jn 12:6)

So the "True Light"—Jesus (see Jn 1)—had appointed a thief as treasurer, and for three years or more, according to John's own account, he had handled the group's finances. The implication here is that Jesus and the twelve were a charitable group, yet there is no record in any of the gospels that Jesus or his disciples ever gave a penny to the poor. We do have the story of the tribute money being given to the temple authorities at Capernaum, but this was purely tactical—as Jesus had only decided to make the contribution "lest we should offend them". The money was produced—abracadabra—from the mouth of a fish (Mt 17:24-7).

Luke omitted the anointing story altogether in case his readers might think that Judas had compassion for the poor, and John retained it while assuring us that Judas' motives were base. The fact that these chronologically later gospels deal with Judas' motivation in this way tells us that they were even then responding to the general question—"Why did he do it?"

We don't hear of Judas again in John's account until Jesus and the disciples have finished dining at an unspecified nocturnal venue the day before the eve of Passover—unlike the synoptics where the dinner takes place on Passover eve itself. Here the devil enters the picture—

> "And supper being ended, the devil, having now put it into the heart of Judas Iscariot, Simon's son, to betray him; Jesus riseth from supper, and laid aside his garments; and took a towel and girded himself." (Jn 13:2–4)

Jesus proceeds to wash the disciples' feet, he tells them they are clean, but—

> "Not all of you. For he knew who should betray him; therefore said he, Ye are not all clean." (v 11)

He tells them how blessed they are and how humble to be, then says—

> "I speak not of you all—I know whom I have chosen—but that the scripture may be fulfilled, He that eateth bread with me has lifted up his heel against me. Now I tell you before it come that, when it is come to pass, ye may believe that I am he." (vs 18-9)

Here he decides to stop beating around the bush and spells it right out—

> "'Verily, verily, I say unto you that one of you shall betray me". Then the disciples looked on one another, uncertain of whom he spoke." (vs 21-2)

The logical thing for them to do now would be to ask Jesus exactly whom he is referring to. Peter is on the alert—

> "Now there was leaning on Jesus' bosom one of his disciples, whom Jesus loved. Simon Peter therefore beckoned to him, that he should ask who it should be of whom he spoke. He, then lying on Jesus' breast, saith unto him, 'Lord, who is it?' Jesus answered, 'He it is, to whom I shall give a sop, when I

have dipped it.' And when he had dipped the sop, he gave it to
Judas Iscariot, the son of Simon." (vs 23-6)

Incredibly, Jesus here appears to be assisting the plans of Satan, who enters
Judas a second time—

"And after the sop, Satan entered into him. Then said Jesus
unto him, 'That thou doest, do it quickly.'" (v 27)

None of this was at all obvious to the others present—

"Now no man at the table knew for what intent he spake this
unto him. For some of them thought, because Judas had the
bag, that Jesus had said unto him, Buy those things that we
have need of for the feast; or, that he should give something to
the poor. He then having received the sop went immediately
out—and it was night." (vs 28–30)

So it didn't occur to one man amongst the eleven to clarify the matter by simply directly asking Jesus where Judas was going. Judas now drops out of the narrative, until his re-appearance for the betrayal scene. Peter obviously didn't press
for an answer to his own question; or perhaps he just lost interest. Even though,
as already stated, neither Jesus nor any of the disciples are recorded as ever giving
money to the poor, John tells us that some of the disciples thought Judas was
going to do *just that*, then and there, breaking from a solemn feast at night time.
Yet a few days earlier, responding to Judas' complaint about the waste of oil, Jesus
had downgraded the need to help the poor as he himself was more important—

"…for the poor ye have always with you; but me ye have not
always." (Jn 12-8)

Let it be noted here that the notion that Judas was treasurer for the group is
derived solely from John's gospel. But the evidence suggests that John created this
occupation for Judas in order to tell us that he was a thief. This was his way of
obliterating the possible motive that could be held up in mitigation of Judas'
behaviour, *viz* that he may have been concerned for the poor. And for those who
might still refuse to be satisfied with the greed motive, he has Satan enter Judas
twice as a back-up measure. In the synoptics, the reader will remember that it

wasn't clear how Judas knew exactly where Jesus would be on the Passover night for the arrest. John has solved this problem—

> "And Judas also, which betrayed him, knew the place, for Jesus oft times resorted hither with his disciples." (Jn 18:2)

This information is unique to John. Why did he bother telling us all this anyway? The answer can only be that he was responding to the problem of "If Judas left the other disciples that night, wouldn't they have noticed him missing?. And if they did, shouldn't they have known that he must be the betrayer. After all, Jesus had made it quite clear that one of them was going to betray him. But then, if Judas had arranged the arrest beforehand, how did he know exactly where Jesus would be late that night?"

John may even have invented the three-year career of Jesus to enhance the possibility that his behaviour might have been so predictable. This could be why he has Jesus appear in Jerusalem early in his career, unlike the synoptics wherein he only goes there just before his arrest—hardly long enough to have established a pattern of sojourning to a particular garden late at night—and wherein his entire ministry seems to be wrapped up in the course of a single year. It should also be noted that, if Jesus posted a guard on Passover eve in order to avoid arrest *a la* synoptics, it was very silly of him to hide from the authorities in his habitual haunt. John, sensibly enough, has jettisoned the story of the posting of the guard!

John's other exculpatory claim—that some of the disciples thought that Jesus had sent Judas out on a late night mission to buy more food for the feast—is particularly weak as John himself told us that the feast had already terminated at the beginning of the same chapter (see Jn 13:2). John was so busy trying to explain why the "Who is the betrayer?" question wasn't followed up that he overlooked the absurdity. To accept John's explanation of Judas' motivation, of course, we have to dismiss the miracles stories in all the gospels. If Jesus could produce food by fiat, as he does in John's "feeding of the five thousand" story for example (Jn 6:9–11), the disciples would hardly have thought it necessary for him to send Judas out to procure food at nighttime. And Judas would be unlikely to sell Jesus out for a mere thirty pieces of silver if Jesus could magically produce money at will like he does in the earlier-cited temple tribute story. John's whole gospel illustrates the difficulties one meets when trying to write the vita of an omnipotent deity who suffers misfortune.

The Jesus/Judas special relationship conspiracy theories grew out of these very problems in the betrayal story. Incidentally, Luke and John's having Satan enter Judas is rather unsatisfactory from a theological point of view. The "Temptation in the Wilderness" episode (missing from John) is usually interpreted as a victory for Jesus as he had withstood the temptation to take possession of all the kingdoms of the world by circumventing the crucifixion. By entering Judas, Satan materially assists the very plan of God that he was supposedly trying to thwart. Jesus is executed and provides the great atoning sacrifice for the whole of mankind. It should have been in the Devil's interests to do what he could to actually *prevent* Jesus being crucified.

So Jesus, by all accounts except Mark's, knew the identity of the betrayer before that person took action. He even told Judas to "do it quickly" and then made no attempt to escape. As the arresting posse knew Jesus anyway, and could have taken him at any time, it was unnecessary for Judas to betray him at all. If Judas were tried in absentia, the case would be thrown out of court. The four "witnesses"—Matthew, Mark, Luke and John—are all manifestly biased in favour of Jesus; and the contradictions and incongruities in their respective accounts would render their testimony unacceptable. The defence would hammer the defendant's lack of tangible motive, and could easily demonstrate the witnesses' transparent attempts to establish one retrospectively.

Suppose for a moment that the gospel accounts of Jesus' fate are just not true. We then face the problem of where the story came from, as intuition would dictate that there must have been an important event around which the tale of betrayal was built, otherwise the gospel writers would not have needed to press-gang ancient scriptures to attempt to explain it. Why should such an internally contradictory story have become the basis for the religion that took over the Roman Empire? Here we should take a look at the events that brought the empire into being.

To Kill a King

Go and tell the Romans that by Heaven's will my Rome shall be capital of the world. Let them know, and teach their children, that no power on earth can stand against Roman arms—Romulus.

As might be expected from so old a civilization, the early history of Rome fades into mythology. Romulus, legendary founder and first king of Rome, united villages, promoted settlement, managed to procure the young Sabine women for his townsmen, created the Senate, the college of Augurs, and executed many other exploits. Or so the story goes. Although usually seen as a benefactor, one theory holds that he was a tyrant and was murdered by the Senate. Seized with panic, his assassins fled from the scene of the crime. An eclipse of the sun and various other celestial phenomena ensued, after which he disappeared in a thick black cloud. He did return to the earth briefly, however, to issue the admonition quoted at the head of this chapter to his follower Senator Julius Proculus. Or so the story goes.

Whatever the facts are, he was later deified under the name of the Etruscan deity, Quirinus. Six kings were to follow till Tarquinius Superbus, regarded as a cruel despot, was expelled from the city by Valerius and Lucius Junius Brutus, the latter becoming famed as the great liberator of Rome. A huge army, mustered in support of Tarquin, invaded Rome, but after some initial success, was finally defeated. Exit the monarchy, the Republic was born.

The whole truth about those far-off days is not ascertainable, but the memory of the tyranny of the ancient kings left a deep imprint in the Roman collective psyche. It became an article of faith amongst the proud republicans that they would never again allow themselves to be ruled by a king. During the following centuries they continued to expand and prosper, surviving onslaughts from the Gauls and Germans, and, having conquered the Carthaginian Empire, spread their influence into Greece and Asia Minor. By the latter part of the second century BC, they held sway over most of the Mediterranean and much of Spain. But all was not rosy in the republican garden. While to some extent democratic, the Senate came to be dominated by about a hundred patrician families, and it took on a reactionary streak. In the course of time two parties had emerged—the Optimates, conservatives who stood for the traditions of the Republic and usually represented the interests of the patricians, and the Populares, radicals who generally represented the plebeians and other classes of citizen. Although Rome was by now a great power, many of its institutions were in a state of decay. The conservative clique in the Senate stood in the way of reform.

Enter Gaius Julius circa 100 BC. The old patrician family he hailed from boasted descent from the ancient Alban kings and the goddess Venus. Although patricians, the family had long allied themselves with the plebeians, believing that the strength of Rome lay with the common people. Julius Caesar's auntie Julia had married the great plebeian leader Gaius Marius, famous for his battles against the Teutons and the Cimbri. His rivalry with the patrician Sulla led to civil war, and he had to flee the city. But when Sulla left Rome with his army to fight Mithridates, Marius took the city, and together with Cinna launched a bloodbath against their opponents.

When Sulla eventually took Rome in 82 BC after the deaths of Marius and Cinna he instituted a bloody regime of revenge that made the excesses of Marius and Cinna look like child's play. He killed so many he was asked to nominate those he would *not* kill so they could breathe easy. Instead he posted proscriptions in the Forum which meant summary execution for those listed. After the reign of terror, Sulla ruled with an iron fist in a titanium glove. The young Julius Caesar had married a girl named Cornelia, daughter of the late Cinna. When Sulla ordered Caesar to divorce her, he refused. Caesar had been appointed *flamen dialis*—priest of Jupiter—by his uncle Marius. Sulla proscribed him, stripped him of his priesthood and confiscated his property. Caesar escaped to the hills, where he slept in caves and shifted from one hiding-place to another, eventually becoming so ill that he nearly died. Sulla's soldiers found him, but he bribed the captain to let him go. In the meantime, his friends, including the Vestal Virgins with whom he was connected through his erstwhile position as priest, were making submissions to Sulla on his behalf. Caesar returned to Rome to stand before him, and, after some prevarication, Sulla pardoned him, while famously remarking "Remember, there are many Mariuses in that man".

To be on the safe side, Caesar decided to leave Rome for a while and set out for the east where he took part in the Roman assault on the Aegean city of Mytilene. During the heat of battle he dragged a wounded comrade to safety, for which he was decorated with the Oak Leaf Crown. He was then sent on a diplomatic mission to Bithynia, where he struck up a friendship—some said a homosexual one—with king Nicomedes, and persuaded him to send a fleet for the

Roman war effort on the coasts of Asia Minor. On hearing of Sulla's death (in 78 BC), he returned to Rome where he set about building his political career. He brought an action for extortion against a former friend of Sulla's, the consul Dolabella, and, although he lost the case, made a mark. He followed this by prosecuting another high official for a similar offence. Again he lost the case, but he had become known for courage and tenacity.

In 75 BC, while sailing for Rhodes to study oratory, he was captured by a band of the pirates who had long terrorised the Mediterranean. They demanded a hefty ransom, but Caesar astonished them by saying that he was worth much more. They happily upped their demand. While waiting for the ransom money, Caesar joined in their sports, read them poetry, and even had the nerve to complain about their raucous partying. He also warned them that once he was free, he would return and crucify them all. They laughed, received their ransom, set him free. He departed, raised a fighting band, returned and fulfilled his promise.

While he was studying in Rhodes, war with Mithridates broke out again. He immediately went to Asia Minor and defended it with volunteers he enlisted himself. During the campaign, news came from his mother that his Uncle Cotta, a member of the College of Pontiffs, had died. The position held power and prestige so Caesar returned to Rome and was successfully elected. He had become quaestor not long before Cornelia died in 68 BC. To do this, he had to borrow a large sum of money from the wealthy property speculator and fire-brigade impresario Crassus, who was famous for putting down the slave revolt led by the gladiator Spartacus—a victory he had consummated by crucifying six thousand slaves along the Appian Way. Caesar's new position was an onerous one, and it was when he was posted in farther Spain that he reportedly grew depressed contemplating a statue of Alexander the Great. At the same age as himself, Alexander had achieved so much, whereas he so little.

Again borrowing from Crassus, he was elected aedile in 65 BC. To make a splash with the common people, he lashed out huge sums for banquets, plays and public games. He engaged so many gladiators for these games that the Senate, fearing that he would use them as a personal army, panicked and restricted the number of combatants allowed. Caesar then raised private funds for major renovation programs in Rome—he was set on being a man of the people. When the *pontifex maximus*, the High Priest of the state religions, died in 63 BC, Caesar—through a combination of bribery and politicking—was elected to the powerful lifelong position. He was the youngest man ever to attain it.

He soon fell foul of the celebrated rhetorician and republican Cicero, who was consul at the time. A number of men had been charged with planning a proletarian coup led by a noble named Catiline. Caesar's spirited defence of the conspirators led to his actually being accused of complicity in the plot, a link that was never established. He sought to save the prisoners from the death penalty, which Cicero insisted upon. Caesar's actions in this case stirred a deep antagonism among many conservative Senators.

In 62 BC he was elected Praetor, just one office inferior to consul. Later that year an incident led to his divorcing his second wife Pompeia, whom he had married shortly after Cornelia died five years earlier. It had been her duty to hold the rites of the Bona Dea (Good Goddess) at his house. These rites, supervised by the Vestal Virgins, were traditionally sacred and restricted to women only. However, Caesar's friend Clodius posed as a woman and joined in the activities. After the scandal Caesar remained friends with Clodius, but repudiated Pompeia, proclaiming "My wife must be above suspicion".

As propraetor of Farther Spain, with an army under his command, he used the taxes raised to repay some of his debts and also curry favour back home by sending money to the State Treasury. An alliance known as the first Triumvirate was formed in 60 BC, when Caesar joined with the wealthy Crassus and Pompey the Great, who was famous both for his conquests in the East and for extirpating pirates from the Mediterranean. Marriage was often a means of underscoring political alliances in those days. Pompey married Caesar's daughter Julia, while Caesar himself married Calpurnia, daughter of the influential senator Piso.

Caesar shared the consulship in 59 BC with a man named Bibulus and so overshadowed him that wags spread the line around that the two consuls for the year were Julius and Caesar. The Senate sought to allot the consuls the supervision of forests in Italy, which Caesar took as an insult. With the aid of the plebeians and his partners in the Triumvirate he managed to secure the provinces of Cisalpine Gaul and Illyricum. He received command of four legions and the right to found colonies. Later, when the governor of Transalpine Gaul died, Pompey insisted that Caesar be allocated that province as well.

Now Caesar was under way with thirty thousand men under his command. From the moment he set out to confront the ferocious tribes to the north and west, he was to spend nine years away from Rome. He was popular with his troops and subdued their fears and won their loyalty via charisma and largesse. In 58 BC he waged successful campaigns against the Helvetii and defeated the armies of the German king Ariovistus. The following year he overcame the Belgic tribes, leading the final charge against the Nervii himself, as they had alarmed his men by catching their javelins and hurling them back. Of sixty thousand Nervian warriors, only five hundred were left alive.

Next year Caesar conquered Brittany and Normandy, and confronted the maritime tribe of the Veneti. Using sickles fixed to long poles, his soldiers subdued them by slashing the rigging of their ships. Although small rebellions kept breaking out, most of Gaul had fallen under his control, and he was already considering an expedition to Britain. In Rome, however, other matters were pressing. News of his fabulous conquests in Gaul made some senators call for celebrations, but others wanted to deprive him of his command. The Triumvirate was in danger of collapsing, so Caesar called Pompey and Crassus to a meeting at Lucca. The conference was successful. Pompey and Crassus were to be joint consuls for the following year, after which Crassus would be governor of Syria, and Pompey of Spain. In fact Pompey ruled Spain by proxy while remaining in Rome himself. Caesar had his proconsulship renewed for another five years.

When Caesar returned to his forces in Gaul, he found that two German tribes—the Tencteri and the Usipetes—had invaded across the Rhine. He claimed that, whilst they had sent envoys to parley with him, their forces set upon his cavalry on their march. When their leaders came the next day seeking a truce he believed they were stalling for more time, so he detained the leaders and marched on their camp and destroyed almost all of them. This was probably the most controversial action of all his campaigns. It enraged his opponents back in Rome, especially the republican Cato, who called for Caesar to be handed over to the Germans.

But Caesar managed to ride out the storm and continued with his military adventures. In a remarkable technological feat, his engineers threw a bridge over the Rhine in ten days. He led his men across, primarily just to intimidate the German tribes into staying on their own side of the river. He had no intention of going any farther at that stage and withdrew to Gaul eighteen days later, destroying the bridge behind him. In 55 BC he sailed for Britain, but it was only a reconnaissance, because he couldn't land the supplies necessary to continue. The following year he returned with five legions and 800 ships. He swayed some local chieftains to his side and fought King Cassivellaunus. However, lack of booty made it unprofitable to stay, so he went back to Gaul.

When his daughter Julia died in childbirth and her baby expired a few days later, his links with Pompey were put under strain. He went on to cross the Rhine again to dissuade the Germans from joining forces with Gauls seeking their assistance. The rest of the year 53 was reasonably quiet and he consolidated his position, finally quashing an uprising led by the Belgic king Ambiorix.

The defeat and death of Crassus at the hands of the Parthians effectively terminated the Triumvirate. Pompey was now seeking the dictatorship of Rome.

But Caesar could do next to nothing politically because he faced a formidable problem in Gaul. The local chieftain Vercingetorix was so successful in spearheading a comprehensive revolt against the Romans that he inspired his countrymen with the hope of invading Rome itself. The rebels scorched the earth as Caesar's forces drove them westwards till they holed up in the town of Bourges. Vercingetorix himself remained outside, but could not cut Caesar's supply lines.

The Romans built ramps and stormed the city, slaughtering the Gauls as they tried to flee through its narrow gates. Vercingetorix retreated to the lofty stronghold of Alesia, which the Romans surrounded, only to be encircled themselves by more Gallic rebels; Caesar was fighting on two fronts against a massive army. The Roman cavalry came to the rescue at the height of the battle. Vercingetorix surrendered, and Caesar threw him in chains. Gaul was now effectively conquered.

In Rome, Caesar's agent Clodius had been murdered, and Pompey was moving closer to the Optimates. Caesar tried to interest him in another political marriage, which he rejected. He was sole consul for 51, and the nervous Optimates were plotting to deprive Caesar of his command. While Caesar considered his options he published his commentaries on the Gallic wars.

From this time on there were many attempts to recall him, but these proposals were vetoed by his tribune supporters. Caesar had shown good faith by sending a legion to Rome for the defence of Syria at the behest of the Senate. Pompey was also asked for a legion, but he recalled the one that he had previously loaned to Caesar. The Syrian emergency passed, and Pompey sent the troops to quarters at Capua, arousing Caesar's suspicions. Caesar's most loyal allies were Gaius Curio and Mark Antony. One of the consuls for the year 50, the nobleman Marcus Marcellus, obtained a resolution in the Senate that Caesar should lay down his command at the due date, but then Curio called for both Caesar and Pompey to quit their commands at the same time. Marcellus moved to put all troops in Italy under Pompey's control. Caesar responded by saying that he and Pompey should relinquish their commands simultaneously. This suggestion was rejected. By then Caesar had reached the southern boundary of his governance at Ravenna. No governor was allowed to bring his troops onto Italian soil without the Senate's permission. When Caesar heard from the Senate that he must lay down his command at the specified date or be declared a public enemy, he sat down near the banks of the Rubicon to ponder his course of action.

The crossing of the Rubicon

Legend says that Pan appeared beside the river and coaxed Caesar's troops to follow him. This was taken as a sign that the gods favoured a crossing, even though it would mean war. "Let the dice fly high!" said Caesar as they set out across the river. He met with little resistance as he was making his way down through Italy. Town after town welcomed him, and many of Pompey's troops deserted to his side. Pompey himself had withdrawn to Campania, and rumours that he had a fleet at Brundisium to take his army to Macedonia demoralized many of the troops who had been left behind in Italy to stem Caesar's advance. The harshness that Caesar had often displayed in his dealings with the Gauls and Germans was not to be shown to Roman citizens. The fortified town of Corfinium attempted to hold out against him. In command there was his bitter enemy Domitius, who had sent urgent messages to Pompey for reinforcements, but was refused them. After a week the besieged troops decided to give up, and delivered Domitius and about fifty notable prisoners to Caesar. These men were naturally fearful as the stories of Caesar's actions in the west were so well known. But to everyone's surprise, he released them all, and told them that they could rejoin Pompey if they so wished. He even gave their troops the pay stored for them in the city.

Pompey's forces sailed to Dyrrachium in the Balkans while Caesar kept the peace lines open. When they were rejected, he turned his attention to Spain, where Pompey's subordinates were still in command. The campaign was short and almost bloodless, the Pompeians surrendering to him in August 49 BC. He was nominated Dictator in Rome, and set out after Pompey, who once more refused his offer of an honourable peace. He claimed he did not want to war against fellow Romans, saying "The war is Pompey's doing. I fight against my own will".

Caesar decisively defeated Pompey's numerically superior forces at the battle of Pharsalus in Thessaly, but Pompey himself fled to Egypt. Once again Caesar pardoned everyone who surrendered. He was presented a bag containing Pompey's papers that included the names of his agents and supporters in Rome, but he had it destroyed without even glancing at its contents. When Pompey arrived in Egypt, the advisers of young King Ptolemy murdered him, vainly thinking that this would curry favour with Caesar, which it did not. He had borne no personal animosity towards Pompey and presumably had desired to renew their friendship in keeping with his plan of reconciliation. On being presented with Pompey's severed head, he was angry and reportedly wept. He had the murderers executed.

He then became embroiled in a struggle between Cleopatra and her brother Ptolemy for the Egyptian throne. In a five-month war, he narrowly escaped death. At one point, besieged by Egyptian forces at Alexandria, he was rescued by reinforcements from Asia Minor, including 1500 Jewish troops under their leader Antipater. The arrival of these soldiers induced the Alexandrian Jews to throw their support behind him, which tipped the balance in his favour and led to Ptolemy's death in battle. Caesar entered Alexandria in triumph in March 47 BC, and installed Cleopatra as Queen of Egypt. A deputation of citizens seeking clemency for their activities in the war came before him, and they too were pardoned.

Caesar's gratitude for the Jewish assistance afforded him can be gauged by his response. He later rewarded Antipater with Roman citizenship, made him governor of all Jewish territories of what was then the province of Syria, and took other measures to protect Jewish rights throughout the Roman sphere of influence—

> "When, therefore, Caesar had overcome his enemies and restored Cleopatra to the Egyptian throne as a Roman ally. He showed marked gratitude toward the Jews. First, he caused Cleopatra to confer some improvement of status (its exact nature is unidentifiable) upon the Jewish community of Alexandria, a measure which was no doubt unpopular with the Greek and Egyptian population, but which could be enforced by the garrison he left behind in the city. The powerful Jewish minorities elsewhere in Egypt, and in other cities throughout the world, benefited as well. Later, he exempted synagogues from a general ban on clubs and other associations. Moreover, he promulgated a series of measures confirming freedom of worship and autonomy for Jewish communities in Phoenicia and Asia Minor. Such decrees were not new, but the extent and detailed character of the edicts attributed to him justify their description as *'a veritable Magna Carta'* guaranteeing the privileges of the Jewish Dispersion." (*The Jews in the Roman World,* M. Grant, 1973, p 59, parentheses and italics his)

Josephus reported that Caesar engraved his decrees concerning the Jews in both Greek and Latin on a pillar erected in Alexandria, and publicly declared the local Jews citizens of that city (*AJ*, XIV, 188). Furthermore, he officially recognized Hyrcanus II as High Priest and prince of the Jewish territories, exempted Jews from military conscription and from paying religious tribute to Rome.

After his conquest of Egypt, he took a leisurely cruise down the Nile with Cleopatra, followed by a flotilla carrying entertainers, dancers and musicians. But Caesar's troops became restless, and he returned to Alexandria. From there he set off to confront Pharnaces, son of the troublesome Mithridates in Asia Minor. After defeating him in a lightning campaign at Zela in 47 BC, he sent his immortal message to the Senate in Rome "Veni, vidi, vici". In October of that year, he returned home to jubilant celebrations. He was now larger-than-life, and his victories had surpassed those of Alexander the Great. In the meantime, some Pompeians had fled to North Africa. They joined forces with King Juba of Numidia, an old enemy of Caesar's, and mustered a large army. Caesar headed for Africa, and as he set foot on the beach he slipped, but maximised the situation by pretending to be kneeling. He grasped the ground and cried "I hold thee fast, Africa!"

His first encounter was with a mainly Numidian force commanded by his former lieutenant, Titus Labienus, who had switched sides during his invasion of Italy in 49. At one point in the battle Caesar grabbed the ensign from his fleeing standard-bearer and exclaimed "Your enemies are in front, not at the back!" He lost this engagement, but retreated safely to his camp under cover of darkness. Then he waited for reinforcements from Sicily before confronting forces under the command of Metellus Scipio. His decisive victory came on April 6th, 46 BC, at Thapsus. He didn't take part in the fighting himself, having suffered a stroke of the "divine madness" of epilepsy the night before. News of the Pompeian defeat triggered the dramatic suicide of the republican stalwart Cato, who had no desire to be pardoned by Caesar, declaring—

> "I am not willing to be indebted to the tyrant for his illegal actions. He is acting contrary to the laws when he pardons men as if he were their master, when he has no sovereignty over them."

Caesar returned to Rome in July, where unprecedented honours were awarded him. He laid on circuses for the people, free food and wine and distributions to the poor. Huge celebrations of his victories were held; he attired in regal purple and gold and riding in a triumphal chariot drawn by four horses. Mindful of the Roman hatred of kings, he chose not to wear the crown of Jupiter, but had a servant hold it above his head instead. He also made a show of humility by ascending the steps to the Capitol on his knees.

He was appointed Dictator for ten years, was made Prefect of Morals, which gave him control over many aspects of Roman social life, and was granted the privilege of sitting in a curule chair in the Senate, being the *pontifex maximus* and all. A statue of him with the globe at his feet was erected on the Capitol. Cleopatra came to Rome with her son Caesarion. In her homeland she was identified with the Egyptian mother-goddess Isis. Caesar opened his new Forum Julium. Earlier in his career he had intended to build a temple in this forum to Venus Victrix, the goddess qua conqueror, but now he dedicated the finished temple to her qua Mother—Venus Genetrix. Of course he himself claimed descent from Venus, and her temple contained two statues, one of himself and the other of Cleopatra. Rome was being pervaded with the oriental aura of divine kings. He drew up plans for the building of roads, canals, theatres and temples to outdo the greatest achievements of Greece and Alexandria. His successor, and first *official* emperor of Rome, Augustus—who later said of the capital "I found a city of stone, and left it a city of marble"—followed the path laid by Caesar—

> "One very important factor in shaping the early development of Augustan architecture was the legacy of ideas inherited from Julius Caesar, at the vigour and versatility of whose vision we cannot cease to marvel." (*Roman Imperial Architecture*. J. B. Ward-Perkins, Penguin, 1981, p 22)

One of his most significant reforms was that of the old calendar, which had become hopelessly out of kilter with the seasons. This he effected in 46 BC, changing it from a lunar to a solar reckoning on the advice of the Alexandrian mathematician Sosigenes. Henceforth, the length of a year would be 365 ¼ days. These quarter days formed a full day at the end of February every leap year. The former fifth month, Quintilus, was later renamed Iulius (July) in his honour. This reform ultimately brought with it the Egyptian seven-day week, which became increasingly accepted so that by the early 2nd century Dio could say that it had become part of Roman "ancestral tradition". The Eastern Orthodox churches still use the Julian calendar today, and in the West it has undergone only minor calibrations to cater for the fact that the true year is about 11 minutes shy of the final quarter day.

Meanwhile back in Spain a formidable Pompeian force had mustered under the command of Labienus and Pompey's two sons. Caesar set out in November 46 BC for what would be his last campaign. It was, according to his own account, the toughest he had ever fought. The gruesome hand-to-hand fighting took place in March 45 BC at Munda and culminated in victory for the Caesarians. Roman settlements were established throughout Iberia, and Caesar was now undisputed master of the whole Mediterranean world. When news of his triumph at Munda reached Rome, the Senate tripped over itself in awarding him new accolades. These, together with what he had already received, were absolutely unprecedented—

> "The honours decreed before Caesar's death went far beyond earlier decrees. He was granted the dress of kings and triumphators for all functions, and the privilege of riding in a chariot and sitting on a golden throne. His statues and attributes were to be carried in the procession of the gods and placed on the couch of the gods in the Circus. His throne and golden crown were to be exhibited in the theatres, his house was granted a pediment, temples were dedicated to him, a flamen appointed, and he was to be called *Jupiter Julius*. He was granted an extraordinary ovatio, treated like a king, and was even offered a diadem." (*DJ*, S Weinstock, 1971, p 270)

The Temple of Clemency

Perhaps because he had personally witnessed and experienced the terrible proscriptions of Sulla as a youth, Caesar had declared that he would not follow his example. While he was warring against the Pompeian forces, some of his supporters in Rome had pulled down the monuments to heroes of the Republic. After he had triumphed at Munda, Caesar had all the statues restituted. He was loathe to openly mock the traditions of the Republic, and his actions in pardoning so many of his bitter enemies amazed the ancient world. Suetonius wrote—

> "Nobody can deny that during the Civil War, and after, he behaved with wonderful restraint and clemency. Whereas Pompey declared that all not actively with him were against him and would treat them as public enemies, Caesar announced that those who were not actively against him were with him. Towards the end of his career, he invited back to Italy all exiles whom he had not yet pardoned, permitting them to hold magistracies and to command armies; and went so far as to restore the statues of Sulla and Pompey, which the city crowds had thrown down and smashed. He also preferred to discourage rather than punish any plots against his life, or any slanders on his name. All that he would do when he detected such plots, or became aware of secret nocturnal meet-

ings, was to announce openly that he knew about them." (Suet *JC*, 75)

Caesar had clearly spelled out his policy early in his Roman campaign. After Corfinium, he had written to his friends in Rome—

> "Our predecessors, by virtue of their cruelty, were not able to escape hatred, and could maintain their victory but for a short time—with the exception of Lucius Sulla, whose model I do not intend to follow. *Let this be the new way of conquering, that we arm ourselves with compassion and liberality*" (*Haec nova sit ratio vincendi, ut misericordia et liberalitate nos muniamus*). How to realise this in very deed is a subject about which I have many thoughts, and there are many ways still to be discovered for its accomplishment." (*Ad Atticum*, Cicero. IX, 7)

An age accustomed to factionalism and bloody revenge provided the stark relief for Caesar's clemency, and this explains the startled tones in which the classical historians comment on it. It is clear that he had often acted savagely in Gaul when he thought exigencies called for it, and no one can forget his treatment of the pirates. But after crossing the Rubicon there was a significant change in his behaviour. When he had escaped from Sulla in his youth to save his life, Sulla's deputy Cornelius Fagita had spared no effort to capture him. Yet when he assumed absolute power—

> "He would not allow anyone to touch a hair of Cornelius Fagita's head, although when he had been ill and a fugitive, he had barely managed to escape from this man's nocturnal ambushes and desire to deliver him into the hands of Sulla." (Suet *JC*, 74)

When Caesar acceded to the will of the Senate and pardoned his intractable opponent Marcus Marcellus who had tried to deprive him of his command, Cicero could not find enough words of praise—

> "...I cannot by any means pass over in silence such great humanity, such unprecedented and unheard-of clemency, such moderation in the exercise of supreme and universal power, such incredible and almost godlike wisdom...But in this glory, O Caius Caesar, which you have just earned, you have no partner...Nay, even that very mistress of all human affairs, Fortune

herself, cannot thrust herself into any participation in that glory; she yields to you; she confesses that it is all your own, your peculiar private desert...to subdue one's inclinations, to master one's angry feelings, to be moderate in the hour of victory, to not merely raise from the ground a prostrate adversary, eminent for noble birth, for genius, and for virtue, but even to increase his previous dignity—they are actions of such a nature, that the man who does them, I do not compare to the most illustrious of men, but I consider equal to God." (*Pro Marcello*)

Velleius Paterculus—

"Caesar returned to Rome when he had conquered his enemies and, *what defies human credence*, he forgave all those who had taken up arms against him." *(Historiae Romanae,* II, 56)

And Pliny the Elder notes that Caesar killed vast numbers in ferocious combat, but assigns to him—

"...the peculiar distinction of the clemency in which (even to the point of subsequent regret) he surpassed all men, *also he afforded an example of magnanimity that no other can parallel.*" (Pliny, Book V11, 93, parentheses his)

The tragedy of Caesar cannot be realised without an awareness of this dimension of his character. To honour this greatest of virtues the Senate decreed the building of the temple *clementia caesaris*, wherein a statue of Caesar would hold hands with the goddess *clementia*, and depictions of this temple appeared on the coinage. But Caesar's head also appeared on the coinage—a privilege formerly reserved only for deceased heroes of the Republic and the ancient gods. Probably the most groundbreaking thing the Senate did was appoint Mark Antony as his personal priest—

"Finally, they addressed him outright as *Jupiter Julius* and ordered a temple to be consecrated to him and his clemency, electing Antony as their priest *like some flamen dialis.*" (Dio *RH*, XLIV, 6)

Cicero clarified the meaning of this in a later polemic against Antony—

"As Jupiter, As Mars, as Quirinus have their priests, so is Mark
Antony priest of the god Julius." (II Phil., 110)

He was further appointed Dictator for Life, granted the honour of being permitted to wear the laurel wreath at all times, and received the title of Liberator.
Statues of him were to be set up in all the temples of Rome and also alongside
those of the dreaded kings of antiquity. Most remarkable was the one to be
placed in the temple of Quirinus—the name of the deified Romulus—bearing
the inscription *"to the invincible god"*. The import of all this cannot be stressed.
The Romans, especially those with republican inclinations, prided themselves on
their rationality. The East was magical, the West pragmatic—

"The East deifies all its masters. Alexander allowed himself to
be turned into a god. His successors followed him. When Caesar was in Alexandria, he saw no objection to letting himself be
proclaimed as a god and a son of a god, and Antony after him
was a new Dionysos for his Eastern subjects." (*The Roman
Spirit*. A Grenier. 1926, p 378).

A monument in the Eastern city of Ephesus already proclaimed in part—

"Gaius Julius Caesar…Chief Priest…God made manifest and
common Saviour of Mankind." (*Corpus Inscriptionum Grae-
carum* 2957 [48/47])

The whole political and social ethos of Rome was being drastically altered. In
a psychoanalytic interpretation of Caesar, Gustav Bychowski wrote—

"There is no doubt that the cult of Caesar became deeply
rooted in the people's psyche and this worship the dictator
sought continually to augment by all possible means. Unquestionably Caesar's real and intrinsic greatness was of material
assistance in this process. Consequently, the old ideals were
slowly replaced in the collective mind by the idea of an Imperator, on whom rested the greatness of the nation and the state."
(*Dictators and Disciples,* Int Uni Press NY, 1948 p 25)

The reality was that although he had not actually been crowned king of Rome,
he already had attained monarchical powers. Exactly whether it was he himself,

or his supporters, or even perhaps his enemies behind the moves to officially make him king is even today a moot point. When the white fillet—symbol of monarchy—appeared on his gold statue on the Rostra, two tribunes of the people had it torn down, saying that he did not need such an adornment. Then, during a festival on the 26th of January 44 BC, he was hailed as king by a crowd as he entered the city on horseback wearing his purple robe and the red boots of the ancient Alban kings. Sensing discontent amongst some, he emphatically declared—

"My name is Caesar, not King!"

But when the same tribunes who had removed the royal fillet arrested those who had hailed him, Caesar's supporters sought to take action against them. Caesar intervened and had the tribunes dismissed. Earlier, he had caused great consternation when, remaining seated while honours were being decreed for him by the Senate, he suggested that his honours should be decreased rather than increased. His opponents portrayed this as an arrogant rebuff to the prestige of the House. Caesar was riding the horns of a dilemma—if he accepted more honours, it would be a sign that he had regal intentions. If he did not, it was proof of his disdain for the Senate. When he became aware of the murmurings against him, he pointedly bared his throat to those around him challenging anyone who would to cut it. Later, it was suggested that he hadn't risen from his chair for fear of possible giddy attacks, but many disbelieved this. His friend Balbus had reportedly said to him—

"What? Do you not remember that you are Caesar, and will you not let them reverence you and do their duties?" (*Life of JC*, Plut)

But the incident that took place at the Lupercalia on the 15th of February was perhaps the clearest sign to his detractors of what his intentions might be. This ancient custom, wherein women flicked by the whips of men running through the streets in wolf skins could look forward to increased fertility, harked back to the mythic origins of Rome wherein Romulus and Remus had been suckled by a she-wolf. Caesar, wearing his purple robe, was seated in the Forum in his golden chair. Mark Antony, his newly nominated priest, raced up to him in wolf skins and placed a crown upon his head. Some cheered, others booed, Caesar removed the crown. Antony offered it several times, and when Caesar persisted in refusing it, the crowd burst into applause. He then ordered the crown placed on the head of Jupiter's statue in the Capitoline, and committed to public record—

"On this day, acting on the wishes of the people, Mark Antony offered Caesar the royal crown, but the dictator refused to accept it."

Obviously, Caesar's refusal of the crown was open to interpretation. Shakespeare has Antony say—

"You all do know that on the Lupercal I thrice presented him the kingly crown which he thrice refused...was this ambition?"

But Shakespeare's Casca—

"I saw Mark Antony offer him a crown; yet 'twas not a crown neither, 'twas one of these coronets; and, as I told you, he put it by once; yet to all that to my thinking he would fain have had it. Then he offered it to him again; but, to my thinking, he was very loath to lay his fingers off it. And then he offered it to him a third time; he put it the third time by. And still as he refused it, the rabblement shouted and clapped their chopped hands and threw up their sweaty night caps, and uttered such a deal of stinking breath because Caesar had refused the crown, that it almost choked Caesar."

But for Caesar's enemies it was all too close for comfort. A plan was brewing to assassinate him. The primary instigator is believed to have been the staunch republican Gaius Cassius Longinus. Other ringleaders were Gaius Trebonius, an ex-consul, and Decimus Brutus—one of Caesar's closest generals. The conspirators thought it essential to enlist the co-operation of Marcus Brutus, a respected praetor who was brother-in-law to Cassius. Brutus had especial status amongst the republicans because he was believed to be descended from the Lucius Junius Brutus held by legend to have driven the last of the tyrant kings from Rome in 509 BC. Involving him in the assassination would invest the act with legitimacy in accord with the traditional Roman belief that regicide was, not merely justified, but honourable. However it was not easy to win Brutus over, because he was close to Caesar and indebted to him. At the battle of Pharsalus, Caesar had sent instructions to the front that if Brutus could not be captured alive he should be allowed to escape. After the defeat, Brutus wrote to Caesar from Larissa seeking clemency for himself and Cassius. Caesar was overjoyed at the news that Brutus was alive and pardoned both men immediately. He had conducted a long-running affair with Brutus' mother Servilia, and there was a persistent rumour that Brutus was actually his son. Not only did he forgive Brutus and many of his friends after Pharsalus, but he also helped establish him as praetor with an expectation of a consulship. It was even considered within the bounds of possibility that Caesar might name Brutus as his successor—he used to address him as "my son".

Notes began to appear on the statues of Brutus' fabled ancestor Lucius bearing messages like "O that Brutus were alive!" or "We need a Brutus today", and in Brutus' own senatorial chair—"Thou sleepest, Brutus, and art indeed no Brutus." Speaking of Caesar, Shakespeare's Cassius says to Brutus—

> "Why, man, he doth bestride the narrow world like a Colossus, and we petty men walk under his huge legs and peep about to find ourselves dishonourable graves. Men at some times are masters of their fates. The fault, dear Brutus, is not in our stars, but in ourselves, that we are underlings. When could they say till now that talked of Rome that her wide walls encompassed but one man? Oh, you and I have heard our fathers say there was a Brutus once who would have brooked the eternal devil to keep his state in Rome as easily as a King."

Tormented by the decision on whether to join the plot or not, Brutus tossed and turned in his bed at night. He awoke to find that his wife Portia had stabbed her thigh in silence. She assured him that if she was capable of this she could keep his dark secret, which he then confided to her. Finally Brutus let his ideological adherence to Roman tradition overcome his gratitude and loyalty to Caesar, and he threw in his lot with the conspirators.

Time was of the essence, as Caesar was due to set off East on the 19th of March to wage war against the Parthians. He was scheduled to attend the Senate on the Ides of March, the 15th, and this was decided as the optimum time and place to do the deed as Caesar would be away from the saluting crowds. Some think Caesar had grown careless. He had dismissed his Spanish bodyguard, declaring that he would rather die than not be able to walk around Rome freely. Of course, the entire Senate had taken an oath to protect his life and many of its members owed their lives to his clemency.

Spurinna the soothsayer had recently warned him to beware the Ides of March. The usual omens reportedly occurred in the last days before the Ides—animals gave birth to freakish offspring, lone scraggly birds wandered in the market place at noon, miracle workers cast fire from unscathed hands etc. On the eve of the Ides, accompanied by Decimus Brutus, Caesar went to supper at the house of Marcus Lepidus. Over wine the topic of conversation at some point turned to death—specifically, which manner of death is to be most desired. Caesar exclaimed—"Let it come swiftly!" Legend has it that later that night he dreamt that he was flying through the heavens holding hands with Jupiter, only to be abruptly awakened as lighting struck the gable of his house, the doors and windows burst open, and the Armour of Mars crashed to the floor. His wife Calpurnia was in the throes of a nightmare, in which she dreamt that his lifeless body lay in her arms.

Caesar was renowned for his fearlessness and placed great store in the goddess of luck Fortuna. But in the morning Calpurnia implored him not to go out of doors that day, to postpone the Senate meeting. On her prompting he went to the auguries, which were decidedly inauspicious. A sacrificed bull reportedly had no heart. Although not given to superstition, he decided to cancel the Senate session. But the fates were on the move. Decimus Brutus, his trusted friend, came to talk him out of it. He told Caesar that it could be interpreted as a mockery if he didn't go to the meeting, as he himself had called it. What would the Senate think if they found out that his reasons for not coming were based on something his wife had dreamt? Furthermore, a prophecy in the Sibylline Books said that the Romans could only conquer Parthia if they were ruled by a king, and Decimus told him that the Senate wanted to proclaim him king of the Roman provinces. Caesar went.

The usual chamber was closed undergoing fire repairs, so the Senate was assembled in the annex of Pompey's Theatre. On the way Caesar met the soothsayer Spurinna, to whom he said "The Ides of March be come", to which Spurinna replied "aye, but not yet past". A man named Artemidorus reportedly handed Caesar a scroll containing a list of the conspirators and their intentions, but hindered by the press of people and the continual salutations, he failed to read it. According to plan, Trebonius detained Mark Antony outside the Theatre. This was Marcus Brutus' idea; the other ringleaders had wanted to kill Antony too, but Brutus insisted that this would muddy the waters and detract from the propriety of their actions.

The Senate rose to its feet as Caesar, wearing the purple robe and adorned with the crown of laurel, entered the theatre and sat down on his golden throne. The conspirators approached the bedecked but affable man, ostensibly with petitions, but in fact they were forming a ring around him to conceal what was about to happen from the rest of the House. A man named Tillius Cimber, kneeling, importuned him for a favour on behalf of his brother. When Caesar told him he would defer his decision on the matter, Cimber signalled his co-conspirators to attack by wrenching Caesar's purple robe down from his shoulder—stripping him of his emperorship. Casca struck first from behind, faltering with a glancing blow just below Caesar's neck. The heretofore-unsuspecting Caesar instantly leapt to his feet, spun around and thrust the assailant away with great force. But Casca cried out for assistance, and within moments Caesar—"invincible in battle-shock"—was being assailed from all sides with only his bare hands to defend himself against the furious onslaught. But the tradition runs deep that what brought him to a halt was seeing Marcus Brutus advancing on him with dagger. In disbelief he uttered his last words "You too, my son?" and, ceasing all resistance, he wrapped himself in his robe and collapsed under a welter of blows. The senatorial onlookers, momentarily transfixed by the horrific spectacle in front of them, fled from the chamber, shortly to be followed by the murderers as well, who ran through the streets with their bloodied daggers proclaiming liberty. The forlorn and mangled body of Gaius Julius Caesar, Father of the Nation, Pontifex Maximus and universal Saviour of Mankind, lay slumped at the foot of the statue of Pompey.

Son of the Gods—Betrayed

Even the lions of Carthage roared their grief at your extinction!

The air was fraught with tension after the murder, with the conspirators nervously trying to wear the mantle of rectitude for killing the man who would be king. They were at pains to assure the populace there was no need for fear, and that the violence would go no further. But the Romans had grown used to the dominance of Caesar, and now he was dead. Some were confused, some were scared, and some were trying to absorb and understand the significance of what had just transpired.

When Mark Antony realised that Caesar was being attacked inside the theatre he had fled, disguised himself as a slave and hidden well into the night. But he was still consul, and by the means of exchanging hostages and using Cicero as mediator, he made contact with the conspirators, and the Senate was convened for an extraordinary meeting before daybreak in the temple of Tellus. A compromise was hammered out between the assassins and the Caesarians. Antony would retain his position as consul, and Cicero persuaded the Senate to grant the assassins amnesty. Antony and Marcus Lepidus even dined with Brutus and Cassius on the Capitoline hill. Although many of the conspirators had wanted to throw Caesar's body unceremoniously into the Tiber, the Senate, at the insistence of his father-in-law Piso, granted him a public funeral as *pontifex maximus*. Furthermore Antony, as his priest, was permitted to make a funeral oration. Marcus Brutus, who had already made a speech justifying the slaying, epitomised thus by Shakespeare—

> "As Caesar loved me, I weep for him; as he was fortunate, I rejoice at it; as he was valiant, I honour him: but, as he was ambitious, I slew him."

—had been alone among the conspirators in not wanting Antony killed along with Caesar. The majority of the cabal had concurred with his authority, but they all watched with some concern as Antony began his speech. He started slowly, and, according to Plutarch, as he noticed in the course of his speech that the crowd was moved when he spoke well of Caesar, he warmed to his theme and slipped from cautious oratory to bold demagogy. He read the will, wherein Caesar had, amongst other things, left a gratuity to every Roman citizen and donated his parks on the banks of the Tiber to public use. These generous acts, combined with the fact that he had pardoned many of his murderers and promoted them to prestigious positions, was to prove intolerable for the people. After listing Caesar's many achievements, military and social, and the extraordinary honours granted him, Antony reminded his listeners that the entire Senate had sworn oaths to protect his life. Dio has him say in part—

> "This alone was enough to prove his goodness, *for he was so truly a son of the gods, that he understood but one thing, to save those who could be saved.* Yet this father, this high priest, this inviolable being, this hero and god, is dead. Alas, not by the violence of some disease, nor wasted by old age, nor wounded abroad in some war, nor caught up inexplicably by some supernatural force, but murdered right here within the walls as the result of a plot…murdered in the Senate house…unarmed—the brave warrior, defenceless—the promoter of peace, the judge—beside the court of justice, slain by the hands of his comrades—he who had so often shown mercy to them! Of what avail, O Caesar, was your humanity, of what avail your inviolability, of what avail the laws? Nay, though you enacted many laws that men might not be killed by their personal foes, yet how mercilessly you yourself were slain by your friends. Woe for the blood-bespattered locks of grey…alas for the rent robe, which you donned, it seems, only to be slain in it!" (Dio *RH,* XLIV, 47-9)

Appian writes that Antony led the mourners like the chorus in a play. Caesar's voice was made to recount all the favours he had bestowed upon each of his assassins, at one point intoning a line from the *Contest for the Arms of Achilles*—

"Did I save these men for them to murder me?"

—and a similar line from Sophocles' *Electra.* In his zeal, Antony paraded Caesar's bloodied robe on the end of a spear, and Shakespeare makes him cry to the crowd that if he had the oratorical skills of a Brutus he would ruffle up their spirits—

> "…and put a tongue in every wound of Caesar that should move the stones of Rome to rise and mutiny!"

Some of the inflamed crowd ran to the murderers' houses to torch them, the servants and neighbours barely managing to dissuade them. Others laid hold of Caesar's body and tried to carry it up to the Capitol for cremation, but were prevented from doing so by soldiers who feared that the nearby temples and theatres might catch fire. So the rioters ripped up whatever they could find combustible in the Forum, hastily built a pyre and cremated the body right there and then. Many were killed in the frenzy. So much had the passions of the mob been fanned in outrage against the assassins that a tribune by the name of Helvius Cinna was mistaken for the praetor and conspirator Cornelius Cinna and torn apart on the spot. In the meantime Caesar's supporters kept vigil at his pyre, and it wasn't just Romans who mourned him. Suetonius reports—

> "At the height of the public grief, a throng of worshippers went about lamenting, each after the fashion of his country; *above all the Jews*, who came flocking to the Forum for several nights in succession." (*JC,* 84)

Briefly, the upshot was that Cassius, Brutus and the other assassins were forced to flee the city. They went to the East and set about raising armies. Antony was left in control of the city of Rome, with the Caesarian forces on his side. Caesar's heir, however, was not Antony but his grandnephew and adopted son, Octavian. At the time he was only eighteen years old and studying Greek literature and rhetoric in Apollonia. On hearing the news, he immediately sailed for Italy. Antony was not pleased. He regarded Octavian as a young upstart and refused to hand over Caesar's inheritance to him. Octavian had to beg and borrow to make good Caesar's legacy to the populace. This engendered much sympathy for him and he drew large numbers of Caesar's troops to his side. Cicero, who now considered it unfortunate that Antony hadn't been killed along with Caesar, persuaded the Senate to send an army against him under the leadership of Octavian and the current consuls. When the consuls were killed, Octavian assumed a consulship and Antony was declared public enemy. Having received official recognition as Caesar's adoptive son, Octavian assumed the name of Gaius Julius Caesar Octavianus.

In the course of time he came to terms with Antony, and in November 43 BC the two united with Lepidus to form the Second Triumvirate. Caesar's magnanimous treatment of his enemies had led to his death, and the three now ruling Rome explicitly declared that they were not about to run the same risk. They brought back the dreaded proscriptions and orchestrated a reign of terror wherein prices were put on the heads of all their conceivable enemies. Relatives and friends betrayed each other in the mayhem that followed, malicious accusations were made, old scores were settled and thousands of innocents lost their lives.

The New God

Caesar now attained in death what he may have been seeking to achieve in life. On the 1st of January 42 BC, the Senate officially deified him as *divus iulius*—the god Julius—an event that only a few short years earlier most Romans would have thought impossible. On earth they slew him because they thought he wanted to be a mere king, now he took his place in the heavens as a god! Thus began the Imperial cult, and the apotheosis of succeeding Roman rulers was to follow. Although Caesar himself had never been proclaimed *divus iulius* in the West during his lifetime, Octavian was not backward when he later allowed himself to be proclaimed *divi filius*—son of the god Julius.

When Antony and Octavian won the second battle of Philippi, Brutus and Cassius committed suicide, the hopes of the Republic dying with them. Then followed another period of rivalry between Antony and Octavian, after which they were again reconciled in the peace of Brundisium. They both set about promoting the cult of Caesar, especially Antony in the Eastern provinces. The longing of the war-weary Romans for stability is reflected in Virgil's Fourth Eclogue wherein the poet proclaims a reign of peace under the beneficent rule of a "peace child"—

> "The final age now has come, foretold in Cumae's song; the great sequence of centuries is being born anew. Now returns the virgin, returns Saturn's reign, now a new generation is sent from heaven on high. On the newborn boy, with whom the Iron Race first shall cease and a Golden Race rise throughout the world, look kindly, chaste Lucina—now your Apollo reigns. Under your consulship, Pollio, this glorious era will start, and the great months begin onward march. Under your leadership all lingering traces of our sin dissolved will release the earth from endless dread. He will receive the life of gods, see divinities and heroes intermingle, and himself be seen of

them; and with ancestral virtues will rule a world at peace. Dear offspring of the gods, Jove's great augmenting seed! Look how the whole vaulted mass of the Universe nods, the land and the oceans' reaches and the deep blue sky! Look how all rejoices in the age to come." (vs 49–52)

But the peace wasn't to be just yet, as Antony and Octavian continued to vie for the authority of Caesar. Antony came to be hailed as a hero at Athens, and in defeating the Parthians, paved the way for Herod the Great to establish himself in Jerusalem. The rivalry between Antony and Octavian broke out again, with Octavian in the superior position. Antony formed an alliance with Cleopatra, but Octavian finally closed in on them. He killed Caesarion in case he grew to become a rival, and Antony, and then Cleopatra, committed suicide.

Augustus Caesar

So the will of Julius Caesar finally triumphed after the tumultuous civil wars precipitated by his assassination. His chosen son and heir was now in firm control, and assumed, through a weakened and compliant Senate, almost total power and the appropriate title of Augustus. He proceeded with a massive building program that included the construction of Caesarea, initiated by Caesar himself, throughout the Roman world for the propagation of the Imperial cult. The knives that had struck at the body of Caesar had effectively killed the Republic itself, and Imperial Rome rose from the ashes of his funeral pyre. Now I want to draw attention to some significant features of this ancient drama.

The impact of Caesar's murder was felt from Gaul to Alexandria, the Roman world was plunged into war and millions of lives were affected. Bizarre reports of unnatural phenomena surrounding this classic story abound. Suetonius reports that in the lead-up to the assassination the "freedom horses" that Caesar consecrated and released when crossing the Rubicon "were beginning to show a repugnance for the pasture and were seen shedding bucketfuls of tears" (*JC*, 81). Roman colonists had reportedly unearthed a scroll that predicted that a "son of Ilium" would be murdered at "great cost" to the body of Italy. Dio claims that Caesar's assassination was followed by "tremendous thunder and furious rain". But the darkening of the sun—in those days regarded as the source of all life—is the most widely attested phenomenon of them all. Mark Antony says it was caused by the murder—

> "...for the sake of which we believe that it was that the sun turned away his light from us, as unwilling to view the horrid crime they (the assassins) were guilty of in the case of Caesar" (*AJ*, XIV, 309)

Manilius—

> "Even the God Caesar fell victim to deceit unspeakable, whereat in horror of the world Phoebus brought darkness and forsook the earth." (Bk II, 595)

Virgil—

> "The sun, too, pitied Rome when Caesar died, and veiled his radiant face in iron-hued darkness, and that impious generation feared eternal night." (1, v 466)

Pliny the Elder—

> "Portentous and protracted eclipses of the sun (do) occur, such as the one after the murder of Caesar the dictator and during the Antonine war which caused almost a whole years continuous gloom" (Bk II, 30)

Plutarch—

> "The brightness of the Sun was darkened, which all through the year rose very pale and shined not out, whereby it gave but little heat. Wherefore the air was rather cloudy and dark by reason of the heat that could not come forth, causing the earth to bring forth but raw and unripe fruit, which rotted before it could ripen." (*Life of Julius Caesar*, 69)

These supernatural reports bear testimony to the powerful sentiments involved here. Plutarch ascribes the demise of Brutus to the workings of divine wrath. Just before the first battle of Philippi, Brutus is alone in his tent—

> "But, above all, the ghost that appeared unto Brutus showed plainly that the gods were offended by the murder of Caesar. Brutus thought he heard a noise at his tent door; and, looking

towards the light of the lamp that waxed very dim, he saw a horrible vision of a man, of a wonderful greatness and dreadful look, which at first made him marvellously afraid. But when he saw that it did him no harm, but just stood by his bedside and said nothing, at length he asked him what he was. The image answered him 'I am thy ill angel, Brutus, and thou shall see me at Philippi.' Then Brutus replied again and said—'Well, I shall see thee then.'" (*Life of JC*, 69)

Valerius Maximus claims that Cassius Longinus also saw the ghost at Philippi—

"Cassius, never to be named without prefix of public parricide, was standing firm and full of ardour at the battle of Philippi when he saw Caesar, majestic beyond human aspect, robed in a purple commander's cloak, charging at him with threatening countenance and horse at the gallop. Terrified at the apparition, Cassius turned in flight from his enemy, first uttering these words: 'What more is a man to do if killing be not enough?'" (Bk 1, 8)

Plutarch says the ghost appeared to Brutus again just before the fateful second battle, this time saying nothing. Brutus took this as an omen of death, and fought recklessly in the vain hope that he might die in battle. The cause was lost. It was only a matter of time. He shook hands with all his men and delivered the last speech of the Republic—

"It rejoices my heart that not one of my friends have failed me in my need, and I do not complain of my fortune, but only for my country's sake. I think myself happier than they that have overcome me; I leave a perpetual fame of our courage and manhood, which our enemies and conquerors shall never attain to; neither by force nor money, nor can they let their posterity say that they, being naughty and unjust men, have slain good men, to usurp tyrannical power not pertaining to them." (*Life of Marcus Brutus*, Plut)

Exit the Traitor

Having said that, he "ran upon a little rock not far off; and there directing the point of his sword against his breast, fell upon it and slew himself." Another version has him throwing himself upon a sword held by his friend, Strato. Now, perhaps because he was rumoured to be Caesar's son, or perhaps because Caesar had taken special measures to ensure that his life was saved after Pharsalus, the name of Brutus came to epitomize treachery. Shakespeare's Antony says of Brutus' blow—

> "This was the most unkindest cut of all; for when the noble
> Caesar saw him stab, ingratitude more strong than traitors'
> arms quite vanquished him, then burst his mighty heart."

The Ides of March was officially decreed the "Day of Parricide"—a parricide being one who kills his father or near relative, one who kills someone sacred, or one who commits treason against his country. The conspirators qualified on all counts, and thereafter it was forbidden for the Senate to convene on that day. Ovid compares the assassins of Caesar with "evil Lycaon" who tried to kill Jupiter when he descended to earth for a reconnaissance on why human society was failing, prompting the deity to destroy mankind by flooding the world in the Greco-Roman version of the Deluge. Putting his case to the celestial Assembly of Gods, Jupiter tells them about Lycaon's treacherous murder attempt, then—

> "The House was troubled at his words, and earnestly required
> to punish he who so traitorously against their Lord conspired.
> Even as when rebels did arise to destroy the Roman name by
> the shedding of our Caesar's blood, the horror of the same did
> pierce the hearts of all mankind, and made the world to
> quake." (*Metamorphoses* I, vs 199–203)

There can be no doubt that the assassins had become fully-fledged deicides. That the perceived perfidy of Brutus in particular was an early development is indicated by a line penned in the name of the 1st century playwright Seneca, where the author has Nero say—

> "Brutus, for the murder of his chief to whom he owed his
> safety, armed his hands. And Caesar, invincible in battle-
> shock, the tamer of nations, walking, a very Jove, along the
> upward path of honours, died by the unspeakable crime of cit-

izens." (*Octavia*, 498–593; from *Three Tragedies*, Harv Uni Press. 1961)

Because the Caesarians won the civil war, it should be little surprise that the name of Brutus sank into obloquy.

The Ascension of Julius

In Ovid's *Murder of Julius Caesar*, Venus is aware of the conspirators' intentions to kill her son. She runs around the heavens trying to corral the other gods into intervening to save him—

> "Look at those evil knives being sharpened! Prevent them, I
> beg you, thwart this attempt, do not allow Vesta's flames to be
> quenched by the blood of her priest!"

But the gods cannot stop the hand of destiny. Heavenly trumpets are sounded, celestial battles fought, the sun refuses to shine, but all to no avail. The agonized Venus is on the point of personally intervening when Jupiter takes hold of her, telling her that the Fates have decreed the crime, but that *Caesar will become an immortal god*. She turns her face from the ghastly murder, but immediately afterwards slips unseen into the Senate chamber and snatches Caesar's soul from his pierced body, transforms it into a fiery star and sets it in the firmament.

Although some folk claimed to have seen the spirit of Caesar rise from his funeral pyre in the form of an eagle ascending into heaven, it really was the comet that appeared in the sky for the seven days of the Circensian games held in July (his month of birth) 44 BC in honour of his victories that was generally accepted as the sign that he had been received by the gods (this was prior to his official deification). The incidence of this comet (not Halley's, as some suppose) was remarkably fortuitous for Caesar's apotheosis, because it was visible in broad daylight and, almost as remarkably, has never returned. It was represented on Roman coins as a star, with the legend *divus iulius*, and an image of it was affixed to the crown on all his statues; it is the origin of the star of divinity that succeeding emperors wore. Horace—

> "The Julian star gleams amid all others like the moon amid
> lesser lights." (Carmen Saeculare 1, 12, 46-8)

And Virgil—

> "Daphnis, why regard the old constellations rising? Lo, Caesar's star has ascended! A star to make the cornfields rejoice in their fruit, to make the grape don its colour on the sun-lit hills." (*Ec* 9, 46-9)

Note the association of the ascending god with bountiful nature. A more poignant *paean* appears in the 5th Eclogue. In *Religion in Virgil* (Clarendon Press, 1935. p188–191), Cyril Bailey identifies Virgil's "Daphnis" as syncretised with Caesar—

> "For Daphnis, cut off by a cruel death, the Nymphs wept (you hazels and brooks are witness to the nymphs). When clasping the pitiful body of her son, his mother shouted the cruelty of both gods and stars. No herdsman in those days drove pastured cattle to the cool rivers, Daphnis; no four-footed beast either tasted a stream or touched a blade of grass, Daphnis. Even the lions of Carthage roared their grief at your extinction! So the wild hills and forests declare." (vs 20–28)

Thus Virgil attests in poetic form to the widely reported view that Nature mourned the death of Caesar. He continues—

> "Daphnis taught mankind to yoke Armenian tigers to the chariot, Daphnis taught man to lead the Bacchic dancers in, and to weave soft foliage around pliant spears. As the vine is the glory of its trees, as grapes are of vines, as bulls of herds, as crops are of fructile fields, you are the whole glory of your folk. Since the Fates took you, Pales herself has quit the land, and even Apollo." (vs. 29–35)

Bailey points out that Caesar had re-introduced the cult of Bacchus; Pales and Apollo are the Italian and Greek pastoral gods, their departure indicating that the flocks have lost their way. The shepherds dedicate a tomb thus—

> "Daphnis was I in the forests, famous from Earth to stars; Guardian of the fair flock, myself more fair than they." (vs. 43-4)

But Menalcas promises—

> "Your Daphnis I will raise to the sky, Daphnis to the stars I'll
> carry, Daphnis loved us, too." (vs 51–52)

He then describes the joy felt as nature comes alive when Caesar arrives at the
celestial abode of the gods—

> "Radiant, he marvels at the strange threshold of Olympus, and
> beneath his feet Daphnis sees the clouds and the stars. At this a
> quickening joy grips forests and country fields, Pan and the
> shepherds too, and the dryad nymphs. No wolf contemplates
> an ambush of the flock, no nets a snare for deer—good Daph-
> nis loves peace. Even the shaggy hills fling with delight their
> voices to the stars; the very rocks and thickets cry aloud—A
> god, a god he is, Menalcas!" (vs. 56–64)

—signifying the mood associated with his ascension, even the fang and claw
regime of nature is seen to abide by his peace. Interesting, too, is what sounds like
annual worship—

> "Whilever boars love the mountain-heights, while fish the
> streams, while bees feed on thyme, while cicadas on the dew,
> always your honour and name and praises will remain. As to
> Bacchus and Ceres, so to you each year the farmers will make
> their vows; and you will bind them to their vows."

All Roman citizens had to make vows to Caesar while he was still living, and
Suetonius reported that a marble column was set up in the Forum after his death
inscribed "to the Father of his Country" where sacrifices were performed, disputes settled and oaths taken in his name (Suet. *JC*, 85).

The New Religion

A complete picture of the exact nature and form that the rituals and ceremonies
of the Caesar cult took on is difficult to establish, but some details are available.
Stefan Weinstock—

> "An altar was set up where the pyre stood in 44; Caesar was
> consecrated in 42 as *divus iulius*; the cult was organised in East
> and West after 40; the temple in Rome was begun in 36 and

dedicated in 29. There were many temples in the provinces, in the first place the Caesarea, partly begun by Caesar himself, then independent temples, no doubt more than we are able to trace, and finally some temples in common with the Dea Roma. His *flamen* became the chief priest of the provinces. The provincial cult was firmly secured owing to the organizational work under Augustus. But the initiative was due to Caesar, not Augustus." (*DJ*, p 309-10)

Mr Weinstock is here responding to the popular perception that Augustus was primarily responsible for the establishment of the Imperial cult. It is often overlooked that Caesar had been the High Priest of all Roman religion since 63 BC, almost twenty years. According to Weinstock, Caesar actively worked on creating a religious cult around himself. In connection with the proliferation of the new cult, he writes—

"His plan was taken up soon after his murder, the cult of *divus iulius* inherited most of its features. It was established everywhere, as well as in the provincial organizations." (op cit., p 143)

The Caesarea built by Caesar himself were in Antioch and Alexandria. There is documentary and monumental proof for the earliest existence of the cult in Corinth—established in Caesar's time—and Ephesus, Philippi, Thessalonica and Smyrna, mostly due to the work of Antony (op cit., p 401-5). The names of these cities might sound familiar to Christians, which brings us to an important question: Should we believe that a religious cult so organised, with such a powerful historical basis and backed by the Roman State—the great superpower of antiquity—could simply vanish without a trace? What I hope to demonstrate now is that this cult, through a strange and arcane process, may have manifested under a different guise. At this point, we must take a further look at the form of Caesar's funeral.

The Funeral Problem

Weinstock thinks that the interval of only three or four days between Caesar's murder and his funeral was too brief for such a detailed event to have been organised, especially considering the confused and tense circumstances that prevailed.

He sees the obsequies as having been planned long before by Caesar himself, and hastily modified to incorporate the murder—

> "It was to be a funeral as never before, like that of Sulla, but with a new fusion of Greek and Roman elements, and above all, including divine honours." (p 354)

Appian claims that Antony, when he had finished his oration, switched to theatrical mode. He gathered up his garments and "raising his hands to heaven in order to testify to Caesar's divine birth" he proceeded to eulogise him. He extolled his exploits and virtues, and—

> "Many other things Antony did in a kind of divine frenzy...(he) mourned and wept as if for a friend who had suffered unjustly, and solemnly vowed that he was willing to give his own life in exchange for Caesar's."

In a state of extreme passion, he lifted the robe from Caesar's body and shook it aloft on the point of a spear—

> "Whereupon the people, *like the chorus in a play*, mourned with him in the most sorrowful manner, and from sorrow became filled again with anger...somewhere from the midst of these lamentations, Caesar himself was supposed to speak, recounting by name his enemies whom he had saved and on whom he had conferred benefits, exclaiming, as if it were in amazement—

> *'O that I should have saved these men to slay me!'"*

Appian writes that the people were again stirred up, then—

> "While they were in this temper and were on the verge of violence, somebody raised above the bier an image of Caesar himself made of wax. It was turned around by a mechanical device, showing the twenty three wounds in all parts of the body and on the face, that had been dealt to him so brutally." (App *CW* II, 146-7)

The reason I mention this is that Weinstock sees problems with repetitions in Appian's record—

> "It is a serious point that Antony first exhibited the robe and then someone else the wax image, both having the same function. We cannot choose between the two items. The robe on the spear corresponds to the robe on the pole in Suetonius' record; and the wax image was an important feature of such funerals, though it had a different function." (*DJ*, p 354)

The robe on the spear was a symbol of the dead Caesar, and the wax image was used at major funerals to represent the body of the deceased. Weinstock objects that the image would not be used to represent Caesar's wounds, nor would it have been rotated mechanically. He suggests that—

> "The difference would be resolved if Appian's record rested not only on the facts of history but also on a *praetexta* called Iulius Caesar. There is no evidence about such a play, but it is not impossible that it existed, considering that there was a *praetexta* by Curiatus Maternus about Cato." (p 354)

This possibility is further enhanced by a glaring contradiction in the historical record. Dio reports that Antony spoke at great length, and provides us with a facsimile of what he said (*RH* XLIV, 36–49). Appian records a longish speech by Antony, delivered with a great deal of histrionics (*CW*, Bk II, 144–147). However, the witness of Suetonius is—

> "Antony dispensed with a formal eulogy, instead he instructed a herald to read, first the recent decree simultaneously voting Caesar all divine and human honours, and then the oath by which the entire Senate had pledged themselves to watch over his safety. *Antony added a very few words of comment.*" (*JC*, 84)

If Suetonius is correct, the lengthy dramatic orations by Antony—in Dio and Appian—might have their provenance in theatrical reproductions of what really transpired. Could it be there was a kind of religious play—a *fabula praetexta*—enacted not only in Rome, but also in the temples of the Caesarea at Antioch and Alexandria, the other cities just cited where the cult was established, and later still in the Caesarea that Augustus built throughout the Roman world? All religions need ritual to survive, and this would have been the ultimate way to promote the cult of the new slain god. And of course the most likely date for this play to have been performed in all its solemnity would originally have been the Ides of March, which, as we have seen, had already been hallowed. Mr Weinstock observes (*DJ*, p 398-9) that during the Perusian war, Octavian fought in the name of the god Caesar, the words "*divom iulium*" adorning the sides of the missiles of his Eleventh Legion. A large number of captive senators and knights were sacrificed at the altar of *divus iulius* on the Ides of March 40 BC—further evidence that the Ides had taken on a strong religious significance.

Being guided by the clearly traceable worship of Caesar before, and particularly *after,* his death, combined with the theatrical nature of the funeral, we can postulate that this religious play—especially if repeated annually—may have evolved to comprise the following essential elements—

1. A great and just man who astounds his age by instituting a comprehensive policy of forgiveness.

2. On the verge of becoming the king, he is betrayed and murdered by those he had saved—the treachery epitomised by his turncoat friend, Brutus.

3. When his tribulation begins, his close friend and religious deputy, sworn to protect him, flees in fear and disguises himself.

4. The murdered man's ultimate triumph, being resurrected as a god.

5. His betrayer commits suicide.

What better foundation "myth" could a religion hope for? It would be difficult to create a fiction that could lend itself more readily to a theatrical presentation. The murder itself was even in a theatre—Pompey's—that was also a "sacred place" (App *CW* II, v 118), in front of an audience—the Senate. Is it not possible that the betrayal and murder of this ancient founder of the Roman Empire, *pontifex maximus* and common Saviour of Mankind, whose name—Caesar; Kaiser; Czar—came to be synonymous with king throughout the Western world, and the shedding of whose blood "pierced the hearts of all mankind", influenced the development of the Christian religion? Is it merely a coincidence that the five points listed above constitute the heart and soul of the Passion of Christ? If we suppose for a moment that the portrayals of the circumstances of the death of Christ as depicted in the gospels are based to some extent *on a play adapted from the Caesar drama,* some important features of Christianity are immediately more intelligible—

1. The spiritual headquarters of Christianity is not Jerusalem, but the eternal city of Rome where Caesar was murdered.

2. According to Catholic tradition, the two most prestigious men in the New Testament, Peter and Paul, both died in Rome, and there Peter had narrated the story of Christ to "Mark"

3. The cities in which we know for certain that the earliest branches of the Caesar cult were established were also all early sites of the Christian church—Alexandria, Antioch, Corinth, Ephesus, Philippi, Thessalonica and Smyrna—as evidenced, amongst others, by the epistles of Paul and Ignatius.

4. The majority of Jews never accepted that Jesus fitted their picture of the Messiah.

5. The title of Pontifex Maximus, which Caesar held for nearly twenty years until his murder—and which was taken up by all the later emperors—merged seamlessly into the title of the Christian Popes as Christianity became the official religion.

6. The significance of the death of Christ is promoted far more than the significance of his life.

7. The Passion of Christ is readily adapted to theatre.

8. The motivation of Judas in betraying Christ has dogged theologians throughout the history of Christendom.

Before looking into how the story of the death of Christ could have come to mirror the death of Caesar, I would direct the reader to the litany of the Good Friday mass, which purportedly commemorates the day of Christ's death. For reasons soon to be dealt with, many aspects of this custom resemble the Jewish Passover, and we find God's laments couched in terms of what he did for his people in Hebrew mytho/history—

God: My people, what have I done to you? How have I offended you? Answer me! I led you out of Egypt, from slavery to freedom, but you led your Saviour to the cross. How have I offended you? Answer me!

People:	Holy is God! Holy and strong! Holy immortal one, have mercy on us!
God:	For forty years I led you safely through the desert. I fed you with manna from heaven, and brought you to a land of plenty, but you led your Saviour to the cross!

(The people repeat their chant)

God continues with declamations such as—

> "What more could I have done for you? I planted you as my fairest vine, but you yielded only bitterness. When I was thirsty you gave me vinegar to drink, and you pierced your Saviour with a lance. I led you from slavery to freedom, and drowned your captors in the sea. I opened the sea before you, but you opened my side with a spear. My people, what have I done to you? How have I offended you? Answer me!"

Appian tells us that the voice of Julius Caesar named his assassins one by one from the funeral pyre, recounting all the benefits that he had conferred on them after pardoning them. In the Good Friday mass, the martyred saviour/god bemoans his execution at the hands of the people he had done so much for. Setting aside the name of the god, the motif is exactly the same—

DID I SAVE YOU ALL FOR YOU TO MURDER ME?

The Passion as Theatre

Some might have difficulty with the concept that Jesus could have stepped into the world from the floor of a stage. Nevertheless the unreal nature of the gospel accounts of his last days is explicable if it was developed from a religious play about Caesar's death. Naturally many variations would have been made, but relics of the play can still be detected.

As a dramatic presentation, much of what is said in a play is rhetorical or thematic. For Jesus to announce that one of his disciples present is going to betray him and then for all of them to ask one after the other "Is it I?" is clearly not a description of reality. One would know if one were going to betray somebody. The notion that all the other disciples would sit idly by as Judas leaves the room, limiting their curiosity to merely asking themselves where he might be going before quickly losing interest in the matter altogether, is an affront to common sense as a history. The scene has been written into the script retrospectively to demonstrate Jesus' omniscience. In theatre the details of a presentation are secondary to the theme being acted out.

The Passion of Christ must have been written before his preceding career had been formulated, for in it he has no miraculous abilities. If he was possessed of magical powers and could transfigure at will, raise the dead, and walk on water etc., why would he need to post a guard to watch out for the temple troopers? And if, on the other hand, he had no intention of avoiding arrest, why would he post a guard in the first place? In the gospels the fact that Jesus is fated to die is presented more as a *fait accompli*—which makes sense if it reflects a historical reality.

Why would Jesus tell his men, who were asleep, to "sleep on now", and then tell them to wake up again in the very next sentence? There is an implied interval of sleep between the two lines, a relic of the ancient version of a curtain fall. Long interstices have no role in a play; an audience doesn't sit waiting for hours as the actors sleep. The problem raised earlier of who could have witnessed Jesus' words while the others were asleep is solved if the words were written and spoken for an audience. Rather than talking meaninglessly to himself, "Jesus" is reminding the congregation that the guards were caught napping i.e.—they failed to protect

Caesar even though they had all sworn to do so. The breaking of that Senatorial oath is mirrored in the gospel accounts of the Last Supper wherein Peter and the disciples earnestly swear not to abandon Jesus.

The events of Passover eve are written like scene changes. The meal at Simon the leper's house in Bethany and the Last Supper were probably originally the same scene, as Mark's 14th chapter doesn't record Judas leaving the room during the Last Supper. As J M Robertson observed, the supper terminates with a hymn, and suddenly we're on the Mount of Olives where another scene takes place, then we abruptly find ourselves in the Garden of Gethsemane, etc. All the gospels follow suit on this. If they were independent historical records, we might have expected some kind of variation in their reports on it. The script of the mystery play must have been gradually understood as a record of real events, and the various editors have added their own clumsy explanations for what would appear to be somewhat irrational behaviour on the part of all the players, as dealt with in chapter one of this book.

Mystery plays about the death of deities are a recognised feature of ancient religion. It is customary for people looking into Christian origins to search for parallels in the stories and legends pertaining to the ancient mythic gods, but they all overlook the god Caesar. Perhaps that's because he is so palpably historical that we have difficulty thinking of him as a god.

The Triumphal Entry

The lead up to the Passion would undoubtedly have been Christ's "triumphal entry" into the Holy City. Caesar, as mentioned earlier, not long before his murder rode into Rome on horseback in the vestments of an ancient king when returning from the Latin Festival at the Alban Mount. This was in accordance with a privilege voted him by the Senate. As he entered the capital, some members of the crowd hailed him as king. He rejected the title with the famous line—

"My name is Caesar, not King"

—but it was received very badly, and his enemies seized upon the event in their justification of his murder (see e.g. Dio *RH,* XLIV, 4, 3–4; 10, 1). Similarly the gospels have Christ being hailed as a king when riding into the capital Jerusalem on a donkey (the donkey has exegetic origins)—an act that is portrayed as signifying his claim to kingship—and similarly his enemies (here the Pharisees) protest the event (Mk 11:2–11). Luke (19:35–40) has the crowd explicitly address him as king—

> "Blessed be *the king* that cometh in the name of the Lord"

When the Pharisees demand that he silence his supporters, Jesus responds with the dramatic—

> "I tell you that if these people should keep their silence the very stones would cry out"

Jesus in this case is boldly affirming the cries of his supporters. The story is represented as engendering the hostility of his enemies, exactly as the historians tell us of Caesar's horseback entry into Rome.

The Last Supper

The meal partaken of at the house of Simon the Leper at Bethany/Last Supper mirrors Caesar's last supper at the house of his heir to the office of chief priest, Mark Lepidus—

> "The day before the meeting (the Ides Senate meeting) Caesar went to dine with Lepidus, his master of horse, taking Decimus Albinus Brutus with him, to drink wine after dinner, *and while the wine went around the conversation*, Caesar proposed the question 'What is the best kind of death?' Various opinions were proffered, but Caesar alone expressed preference for a sudden death. In this way he foretold his own end, and conversed about what was to happen on the morrow." (App *CW* II, 115)

Accordingly, in the gospel, Jesus passes the wine around after supper and foretells his own death on the morrow as he addresses those present. There were two Brutuses close to Caesar involved in his betrayal—Marcus and Brutus—and perhaps John also mirrors this when he tells us that there were two Judases intimate to Jesus at the fateful supper (see Jn 14:22). Luke also reports two Judases as intimates of Jesus (Lk 6:16).

The Denial

The question raised in chapter one of this book—as to why Peter's interrogators made no attempt to arrest him after he broke down and wept—is answered if the famous "denial of Christ" scene masks Antony's abandonment of Caesar in his moment of peril. Antony and Peter are the appointed priests of their respective deities. Before the battle of Actium, Octavian's propagandists had to build a picture of Antony's perfidy in order to justify their intended civil war against him. After the battle of Actium and the suicide of Antony it would have been perfectly in Octavian/Augustus' interests to allow the perceived cowardice of Antony in abandoning Caesar to be incorporated into the rites of the cult. His birthday had been declared *dies vitiosus*—a sinister day. When the young Octavian had first come back to Rome after Caesar's murder, he had confronted Antony about the deals same had made with Caesar's assassins. Now that the *flamen* Antony no longer existed and, after Lepidus died (ca 12 BC), Augustus assumed the office of *pontifex maximus*, he was in a perfect position to resurrect the scandal and institutionalise it in the liturgy of the cult.

But at the same time Antony still had to be recognised and honoured for his assiduous work, as Caesar's first priest, in spreading the cult. This simultaneous despising and honouring seems to have been a Roman trait, as evidenced in the character of their ancestral gods. Antony's pivotal role could not simply be blotted out from the annals of the cult. Christian apologists often claim historicity for this story of Peter's denial of his master, their reasoning being that the Christian scribes would not want to record such a failure of duty by the first ordained priest of Christ—and here I would agree with them, only they have lost sight of the historical basis. Peter's denial in the gospels is purely thematic; it has no consequence, as we saw. These two features of the Passion, the betrayal and the denial, are always emphasised in re-enactments and liturgical readings.

The traitor takes his life

The book of Acts tells us of the suicide of Judas—

> "Now this man purchased a field with the reward of iniquity;
> and falling headlong, he burst asunder in the midst, and all his
> bowels gushed out." (Acts 1:18)

We noted before that Marcus Brutus either threw himself forwards onto his own sword, or threw himself forwards onto his sword held by Strato. In either case, he fell frontward and his innards would have presumably "gushed out". The gospels offer us nothing more than a seizure of inexplicable remorse as a motive for this act of Judas, whereas for Brutus his entire *raison d'etre* had been snatched away.

New life for ancient ritual

As mooted earlier, the underlying *structural* theme in the Passion of Christ is that of the dying saviour/god. This is an ancient religious motif in the Levantine, and is embodied in the rites of such pagan deities as Tammuz, Adonis and especially Attis. These gods died annually as Christ continues to do, and were annually lamented by a goddess or a troop of women. It will be remembered that the theme of the weeping goddess features in Virgil's *paean* to the murdered Caesar—

> "When clasping the pitiful body of her son, his mother
> shouted the cruelty of both gods and stars." (*Ec* 5, 24)

This "mother" was the goddess Venus, who, as Ovid tells us, immediately seized Caesar's soul after his murder and carried it to the realm of the gods. And of course, this is the classic model of the Christian *pieta*, wherein the mourning Virgin/Mother has her lifeless divine son draped over her lap.

To paraphrase Sir James Frazer's theory, in very early times these dying/resurrecting god cults probably involved the sacrifice of a young man at cardinal points of the year, principally around the northern spring equinox (Easter/Passover etc). Obviously agrarian peoples wanted bountiful crops and besought them from their gods, and these human sacrifices were a kind of sympathetic magic rooted in the belief that the vigour of the slain man would be translated into the growth of the crops for the coming season. Salvation was earthly and tribal, the individual counted for very little outside of being a vehicle for the perpetuation of the race (today we might call it the gene). But with the detribalisation concomitant with advancing civilisation the idea of salvation of the tribe evolved into the more individualistic one of personal existence in the hereafter. The human sacrifices were gradually phased out, and the god would either be killed in effigy, or the theme of his death and resurrection would merely be reflected in the cult's litany. Even in the OT there are traces of such practices being observed at the temple in Jerusalem—

> "Then he (the Lord) brought me to the door of the gate of the
> Lord's house which was towards the north; and behold!—There
> sat women weeping for Tammuz." (Ezek 8:14)

Naturally 'the Lord" describes this practice as an abomination, for Tammuz was the Babylonian version of the annually dying god. Much of the OT deals with the problems that the chief Hebrew deity had in keeping his people from engaging in foreign cultic practices, and they are constantly exhorted to keep to their own religious customs. These repeated demands for strict obedience suggest that other beliefs and practices were widespread. The tradition of the pierced or speared god hanging on a tree was far flung, stretching from the Levant to northwest Europe—

> *"I know that I hung on the windswept tree*
> *For nine whole nights*
> *Wounded with the spear, dedicated to Odin*
> *Myself to myself".*

These words are from the Havamal, and are part of the rites of the Norse god Odin, the "God of the Hanged". Odin laments "they did not comfort me with bread, nor with the drinking horn". He then screeches on the brink of death, grasps the mystic runes, and becomes one with the "world-tree". The notion that the spirits of the lamented dead would return in the plants and trees was widely held. The Greeks thought that water lilies were the spirits of maidens who died in youth, and the Syrians believed the violets to have sprung from the blood that dripped from the wounds of Attis. Similar beliefs can be found as far afield as amongst the Aborigines of Australia.

In respect of the rites of Adonis, Sir James Frazer suggested that the deity may sometimes have been personated by a living man who died a violent death in the character of a god, and that the blood and spirit of those horribly murdered was believed to empurple or incarnadine the flowers. He cites from Omar Khayyam's Rubaiyat—

> *I sometimes think that never blows so red*
> *The rose as where some buried Caesar bled,*

That every Hyacinth the garden wears
Dropped in her lap from some once-lovely head.
And this reviving herb whose tender green
Fledges the river-lip on which we lean-
Ah, lean upon it lightly, for who knows
From what once lovely lip it springs unseen?

We have already seen testimony—both from poets and historians—of the impact that Caesar's murder was perceived to have on nature, and he *was* slain in the character of a god. Did his death breathe new life into these ancient dying/resurrecting god customs? Poetic allusions to his blood suffusing the earth and nature springing to life at his ascension would suggest so. And the timing and circumstances of his death could not have been more propitious for such an eventuality. There are very good reasons why a mystery play based on his murder *and* incorporating the dying/resurrecting god theme might have been created—

1. He died in the religious role of High Priest and a deity, Jupiter Julius, in a "sacred place" (App *CW* II, 118), in a ritualistic killing (all the conspirators had to strike him).

2. As noted, he was murdered in a theatre (the annex of Pompey's Theatre) in front of an audience (the seated Senate)—factors which would readily lend themselves to a theatrical reproduction.

3. The Ides of March (15th) was later hallowed as the "Day of Parricide", a day on which the Senate was forbidden to meet, and it is likely that a solemn annual memorial would have taken place in the temples which had been constructed throughout the Roman sphere of influence for the promulgation of the new religion.

Now the Ides of March just happened to coincide with the solemn beginning of the festival of the mysteries of Attis, an extremely popular annually dying god who had been imported into Rome from Phrygia—central Turkey today. The calendar came to be constituted of the following—

March 15—*canna intrat*—procession of the reed-blowers.

March 22 (northern spring equinox)—*arbor intrat*—burial of Attis in effigy, adorned with flowers, affixed to a pine tree or stake.

March 24—*sanguis*—day of mourning, sacrifice, and bloodletting.

March 25—*hilaria*—joyous resurrection of the god.

March 27—*lavatio*—day of holy ablution.

Here we see the pre-Christian Easter formula replete with a three-day schedule between the burial of the deity and his resurrection. The inclusion of the Hilaria as the day of Attis' resurrection is disputed, because the earliest references to the cult display a more matriarchal orientation towards the interests of his mother Cybele. The 25th of March is three days after the northern spring equinox, and follows three months from the similar linkage between the northern winter solstice on the 22nd of December (as it was calculated) and the culmination of the Saturnalia three days later on the 25th—the day of the birth of Christ in our own mythology. It is not normal for people to re-enact funerals for mere mortals, although they may hold a memorial day, an anniversary or a day of meditation. (The Christian festival is still a re-enactment; the Easter Sunday proclamation is not "this is the day that Jesus rose" but "Jesus *is* risen".) In the case of Attis, the *arbor intrat* is not disputed, and in view of the fact that Attis is represented on vases as prostrate dying under the tree in one scene, juxtaposed with him dancing in the next, from as far back as the 4th Century BC, it is not unreasonable to assume that he must have been regarded as returning to life. An atavistic association of Attis' resurrecting with dancing may even be the subconscious source for the words of the Christian ditty—

> *I danced on a Friday when the sky turned black*
> *It's hard to dance with the devil on your back*
> *They buried my body and they thought I'd gone*
> *But I am the dance and the dance goes on.*
> *Dance, dance, wherever you may be*
> *I am the Lord of the Dance said he*

And I'll lead you all, wherever you may be
And I'll lead you all in the dance said he

Christian critics are quick to point out that in some legends Attis dies and remains dead, and they present his annual burial as proof of his enduring deadness. However, the death of Christ is also mourned annually, which is consistent with its ritual source in the same cycle of nature. The earliest records of the Western church indicate that Christ's resurrection was celebrated in Rome on the same date annually—March 25th, the Eastern churches celebrating it on the spring festival of Passover. The blooming of spring was regarded as the natural beginning of the year. March 25th was New Year' Day, indulged in with due mirth and hilarity in the Roman world until Pope Gregory officially referred it back to January 1st in 1582. It should surprise no one that the Protestant English authorities would not recognise Gregory's reforms until 1752. The reality, of course, consistent with what we know about the difficulty of changing inveterate custom, is that the common people would have been increasingly celebrating Caesar's New Year—the day on which he was officially deified—one custom gradually eclipsing the other over a long period before Gregory ratified it.

The festive calendar of Attis was incorporated into Roman state religion in the reign of the emperor Claudius in the fifth decade of our era, around the time of the emergence of embryonic Christianity. We should consider the possibility that Caesar's ascension could have influenced both belief systems, effecting a greater emphasis on resurrection (I will shortly demonstrate that the earliest Christian epistles show varying levels of interest in the phenomenon). Claudius would presumably have given the Attis festival the state imprimatur in order to take control of what was a growing religious practice. Previously the priests of the cult, the Galli, had all been Phrygian eunuchs. Claudius made a number of reforms to the festival, decreeing, for example, that the priests of the cult would in the future have to be Romans. Claudius' intention would have been to suppress or stamp out the more extreme practices of the cult, such as the atavistic bloodletting on the 24th of March, which sometimes included whipping and auto-castration. It should be noted here that there are parts of the world where Christian sects still engage in flagellation, self-harm and bloodletting—notably in the Philippines, where some of the more enthusiastic devotees affix themselves to crucifixes at Easter, the premium being on suffering.

The Attis festival began on the 15th of March with performances by a special class of reed-blowers to lament the hapless deity, who had sacrificed himself via castration and bled to death slumped backwards against a pine tree. As this was the first day of the commemoration, it was presumably believed that this was the day that Attis had actually died. But this day was also the hallowed Day of Parricide, and had been since 44 BC, giving the common people plenty of time to come to interpret the mourning reed-blowers as lamenting the loss of Caesar. This would seem to be of particular relevance to the Roman Jews, as they would no doubt identify the Ides of March with their own solemn festival of Passover, which falls on the 15th of their overlapping month of Nisan, and often would have fallen within the spring religious festival. Here we can see precisely how Julius Caesar's death could have been religiously entwined with a ritualistic burial of the deity followed three days later by the celebration of his resurrection. Indeed it would be a remarkable thing if the three commemorative rituals had not been confused. The first century of our era is renowned as the great age of syncretism.

Julius Caesar—friend of the Jews

It was noted above that Suetonius claimed the Jews were the most assiduous mourners at Caesar's funeral. There are especial reasons for this. From an early time he had regarded the Jews in Rome—with their self-sustaining communities—as an important contribution to Roman stability. At the time of his early career, Rome had maintained an alliance with the Jewish kingdom for over a hundred years. It was also noted that Caesar, in gratitude for the Jewish assistance that he received in Alexandria, had issued a plethora of decrees protecting Jewish religious and civil rights throughout the Roman domain. Here is a typical one amidst the list provided by Josephus—

> "Julius Gaius (Caesar), consul of Rome, to the magistrates, senate, and people of the Parians, sendeth greeting. The Jews of Delos, and some other Jews that sojourn there, in the presence of your ambassadors, signified to us that, by a decree of yours, you forbid them to practise the customs of their forefathers, and their way of sacred worship. Now it does not please me that such decrees should be made against these our friends and confederates, whereby they are forbidden to live according to their own customs, or to bring in contributions for common suppers and holy festivals…It will therefore be good for you, that if you have made any decree against these our friends and confederates, to abrogate the same, by reason of their virtue and kind disposition towards us." (*AJ*, XIV, 213-6)

Although the Romans had an overall tradition of religious tolerance, Caesar's special favour for the Jews set the stage for his followers to maintain it. The fact that Caesar's generally pro-Jewish policy was sustained is all the more remarkable because most of the references to the Jews by Caesar's contemporaries tend to be negative or even derogatory. Jews in Rome bitterly lamented the death of the high priest Caesar at a funeral that was religiously organised, and many of those Jews were from other parts of the nascent Roman Empire. Those sceptical that Jews could regard the non-Jew Caesar as messianic should consider the precedent of the Persian Cyrus the Great. After defeating the Babylonians in the 6th century BC and liberating the captive Jews, he permitted them to return to their homeland and rebuild their temple. He is described in Hebrew scripture as the servant of God (Ezra 1), and referred to in Isaiah 45:1 as "the Lord's anointed"—the "anointed one" being the meaning of Messiah or Christ. One of the most common titles for Caesar, on inscriptions throughout the Empire, was "Saviour", which is one of the meanings of Yehoshua (Joshua, Jesus); "Christ Jesus" approximates to "anointed saviour".

Caesar had other messianic qualifications from the Jewish point of view. His opponent Pompey the Great had defiled the temple in Jerusalem by entering the Holy of Holies, and consequently his demise was called for, and then described, in Psalm 2 of the *Psalms of Solomon*—(aka the *Psalms of the Pharisees*). The psalmist calls on God to arise and defeat him. This is from an early commentary by Herbert Ryle and Montague James—

> "The 'sinful man' (v1) 'the dragon' (v 29) whose purpose had been to rule the world, who had set his 'greatness' against that of God (33), is pierced and slain in Egypt (30), his body lies neglected, unburied, on the waves (30, 31). This description agrees closely with the fate of Pompey. He made a bid for supreme power against Caesar; he was surnamed 'the Great'. He was treacherously assassinated on the shores of Egypt (Sept. 28, 48 BC). The overthrow of the oppressor heralds the triumph of the lowly (v 35). It is worth noting that while, as appears from this Psalm, the Jews regarded Pompey as a tyrant, they glorified Caesar on account of his clemency and consideration toward their own race. The concluding burst of triumph in our Psalm probably indicates the satisfaction of the patriot Jews at the complete success of Caesar's arms. After arranging matters in Egypt, and overthrowing Pharnaces, king of Pontus, with extraordinary suddenness, he returned to Syria, and in

July of 47 was in Antioch, making provision for the good gov-
ernment of the province of Syria and dispensing favours to the
states who had supported him during his recent campaign. The
special privileges that he awarded to the Jews are recorded in
Jos. Ant. XIV. x, 1–10." (Cambridge Uni Press, 1891)

So Pompey, setting his "greatness" against God, was thoroughly vanquished
by Caesar, who subsequently issued a raft of decrees protecting Jewish religious
rights. Further, Caesar's assassin and Pompey supporter Cassius Longinus had
aroused the hatred of many Jews by selling the inhabitants of the Jewish towns
Gophna, Emmaus, Lydia and Thamna into slavery (*AJ*, XIV, 271-6). And Caesar
had been due to set off on the 19th of March to wage war on the Parthians, who
had become a source of anxiety to the oriental Jews. Cassius' leading role in Caesar's assassination would have exacerbated their sense of grief.

Finding prophecies in the Hebrew scriptures to establish Caesar's messianic
credentials would have presented little problem. Hugh Schonfield claims that
ancient apocalyptic Jewish students of scripture had calculated that the "last days"
would begin sometime after 46 BC, and that many Jews expected the messiah to
appear soon after that date (see *The Passover Plot,* p 23). This calculation was
based on applying the exegetic day-for-a-year principle to the "seventy weeks"
prophecy of Daniel 9:24-7; whereby 490 years was interpreted as needing to
expire from the time of the decree of Cyrus the Great to rebuild the Jerusalem
temple till the coming of the Messiah. Daniel's text says that after this time
"…the messiah shall be cut off, but not for himself". Naturally, Christianity
interprets this as referring to the killing of Jesus Christ, but both the timing and
manner of Caesar's death fit the text much more closely. It must be borne in
mind that the matter of whether "Jesus of Nazareth" filled the prescription better
could not have been an issue when Caesar was slain in 44 BC.

Another messianic Hebrew text, later applied to Jesus, appears in Zechariah
13:6—

"And one shall say unto him, What are these scars in thine
hands? Then he shall answer, '*Those with which I was wounded
in the house of my friends*'."

It was well known that Caesar was unarmed when he was attacked by the
assassins' knives, and had to defend himself with his bare hands. According to
some accounts, it was the sight of the dreadful scars on the wax image of his body
at his funeral that enraged the mob against the assassins. And Caesar *was* slain in

the house of his friends, as intoned in the funeral speech by his "flamen dialis" Antony—"...*in the Senate house...how mercilessly you yourself were slain by your friends*". Even the statue of Pompey that kept silent vigil over the gruesome act, and at the pedestal of which Caesar fell, had been ordered rebuilt by him as part of his policy of reconciliation.

The Hebrew tradition that a messianic figure would be slain by piercing or stabbing was widely extant, as yet another text from Zechariah that is often applied to Jesus indicates—

> "...and they shall look upon me *whom they have pierced,* and they shall mourn for him, as one mourneth for his only son, and shall be in bitterness for him, as one that is in bitterness for his firstborn." (Zech 12:10)

If the mourning Jews linked these prophecies with the traditions of the "Suffering Servant" (SS), Caesar could be regarded as fulfilling the expectations of the messiah. It is well known that the SS material is the main literary (as opposed to historical) source for the gospel depiction of the Passion of Christ, and at this point it is worth quoting it *in toto*—

> 1. Behold, My Servant shall deal prudently, he shall be exalted and extolled and be very high. Just as many were astonished at you, so his visage was marred more than any man, and his form more than the sons of men; thus shall he startle many nations. Kings shall shut their mouths before him; for what they knew not of they shall see, and what they had not heard they shall consider.

> 2. Who has believed our report? And to whom has the arm of the Lord been revealed? For he shall grow up before him as a tender plant and as a root out of dry ground. He has no form or comeliness; and when we see him, there is no beauty that we should desire him. He is despised and rejected by men, a man of sorrows and acquainted with grief. And we hid, as it were, our faces from him; he was despised and we did not esteem him.

> 3. Surely he has borne our griefs and carried our sorrows; smitten by God and afflicted. But he was wounded for our transgressions, he was bruised for our iniquities; the chastisement for our peace was upon him and by his stripes we are healed. All we like sheep have gone astray; we have turned, every one, to his own way; and

the Lord has laid on him the iniquity of us all. And he, because of his affliction, opened not his mouth: he was led as a sheep to the slaughter, and as a lamb before the shearer is dumb, so he opens not his mouth. In his humiliation his judgment was taken away: who shall declare his generation? For his life is taken away from the earth: because of the iniquities of my people he was led to death. And I will give the wicked for his burial, and the rich for his death, for he practised no iniquity, nor craft with his mouth. Yet it pleased the Lord to bruise him; he has put him to grief. When you make his soul an offering for sin, he shall see his seed, he shall prolong his days and the pleasure of the Lord shall prosper in his hand. He shall see the travail of his soul and be satisfied. By his knowledge my righteous Servant shall justify many, for he shall bear their iniquities, therefore I will divide him a portion with the great and he shall divide the spoil with the strong, because he poured out his soul unto death and he was numbered with the transgressors, and he bare the sin of many and made intercession for the transgressors." (Isaiah 52:13–53:12)

The above divisions of the text are my own, in order to illustrate that: Section (1) talks about the greatness of the man in the earthly realms, and then it adumbrates his death in terms of physical mutilation—*his visage was marred more than any man, and his form more than the sons of men*—then proceeds to tell us that *kings shall stop their mouths at him*—a description of his overarching dominance, representing a return by the author to the temporal sphere. Section (2) is essentially a lament—expressed in hyperbolic terminology—that (we) did not recognise him for who he was. Section (3) presupposes his slaughter/sacrifice, and describes his posthumous greatness and soteriological significance.

Many aspects of this description are fulfilled in Caesar—he deals prudently, he is exalted and extolled, at some point he is rejected, he is led like a lamb to the slaughter (Brutus "*took him by the hand and led him to the Senate*", see Plut *Caesar* 64, 4), his life is taken away from the earth, he is posthumously deified "therefore I will divide him a portion with the great". (Shortly I will demonstrate that the above SS description seems to be just about all the biographical detail of the life of Christ known to the earliest Christian writers—who wrote long before our gospels appeared.) I am not suggesting that all Jews would have regarded Caesar in this light, but there almost undoubtedly would have been a Jewish wing of the Caesar cult, even if it were originally only a minority movement. All the signposts point in that direction. Judaism was a much broader church than most people suppose, and Jews were diffused throughout the Roman domain, comprising around ten percent of the general population. Suetonius reported that they lamented Caesar "after the fashion of their country", meaning their culture—and an essential part of that culture was a thirst for prophecy and exegesis. Students of prophecy will understand that Caesar does not need to fulfil every jot and tittle of the Isaiahan text—having been a real person his life could not be prescribed by an oracle—but just enough for him to be identified with it. And the circumstances of his death attract that identification on many fronts. The ides of every month was dedicated to Jupiter, and a white lamb—*ovis idulis*—was led along the Via Sacra in Rome to be sacrificed at the temple of Jupiter—the greatest of the Roman gods and one with whom Caesar, while still living, had been officially identified as *iupiter iulius*. Nicholas of Damascus reported that Caesar's body had been ferried home to his residence along the Via Sacra to be met by his weeping household. This alone is enough to occasion his identification with the Passover lamb—especially if the 15th of March and the 15th of Nisan were close together in that year. Caesar had been led like the *ovis idulis* to the slaughter *a la* SS. Note that the Servant's death is portrayed in sacrificial and expiatory terms, he "poured out his soul unto death", and "he bare the sins of many". There is no dispute that these were raw ingredients for the development of the soteriology of Christianity.

If an oriental Jewish branch of the Caesar cult originally observed commemorative readings of the Isaiahan text on the Ides of March, the custom would have fairly soon been referred to the appropriately solemn occasion of Passover itself, which already involved the sacrifice of a lamb. This is just the way that the perceived death of a god like Julius could enthuse existing customs. The Jews would have needed to interpret what this meant for them in the light of their own religious traditions, and their reverence for Caesar may have inspired them, over time, to write a Judaic version of the commemoration in terms that their Jewish congregations could relate to, grafting its tragic elements onto their existing liturgical expressions of the Passover SS and their messianic traditions. For a long period of time, the Jewish sect may have commemorated Caesar's death in this Judaic guise, Caesar as Jupiter being replaced by the Hebrew equivalent Yahweh in an honorary capacity. The names of these two deities are basically the same. The form of the Roman oath "by Jupiter" (or as we rather say "by Jove"), is *iove*—pronounced "yo way" in Latin, as compared to the Hebrew "ya way". This is a sound explanation for why the litany of the Good Friday mass is a blending of the Jewish Passover with the theme of Caesar's funeral—"I opened the Red Sea before you, but you opened my side with a spear" etc. Note that the OT God (the Father) refers to Christ's death as his own—as if the father Jupiter were refer-ring to his "son"—Jupiter Julius.

Such a Jewish cult, with the trauma over the loss of Caesar waning with the passing of time, would drift away from the more orthodox *divus iulius* cult, but retain the Judaic commemorative reading and litany as described above. With further passing of time, two or three generations, the consciousness that the com-memorative reading had been inspired by the fate of Caesar would fade, and the laity would come to accept that the *SS himself* had been a real character—typol-ogy being misunderstood as chronology. The commemoration proper would be the vehicle to carry the religion rather than the biography of the deity. Christ's breaking of the bonds of death could be regarded as a *fait accompli* by way of a cultic interpretation of the coincidental celebration of Hilaria. Such an evolution-ary development is not inconsistent with the facts that can be established about early Christianity. (I shall demonstrate later that the message of the early Chris-tian apostles was not that Christ had *just recently* risen from the dead, but rather that God had recently *confirmed* that he indeed at some point had, and that he is "coming" soon).

As the religion would grow with the passing of further time, more aspects of Caesar's tragedy would leak through the cusp into the commemorations of the death of Christ, consciously or unconsciously. Significantly, the Latin word for assassin is "sicarius"—from *sica*, meaning dagger. In the posited Caesarian play Brutus the assassin would be "Brutus sicarius". Now Isaiah has the SS smitten for his people—the Jews—and the term Jew is derived from their traditional patri-arch—as we say "Judas"—and was perhaps the most common name of male Jews at that period of history.

Et tu, Judas?

If the SS is smitten on behalf of the Jews, it is not a far cry to say that the Jews were responsible for his death. So why not refer to the betrayer as "Judas sicar-ius", so that the assassin takes on the eponymous name of the people the SS dies for? In translation, or with the passing of time, the description "sicarius" could have been understood as the name of the character involved (in the same way that some people think "Christ" is the surname of Jesus) and corrupted to *Judas Iscar-iot*. This interpretation of the name *iscariot* has wide acceptance amongst etymol-ogists, and is the principal reason for the development of the mainstream occultist view that Judas Iscariot was a dagger-toting Zealot, a *sicarius*. His role in our gospels is only to betray Jesus to the authorities, but I would suggest that in an earlier version his full role could have been exactly what his name implies; he would stab Jesus with his dagger, after which Jesus would be hanged on a tree, stake, or cross, buried (*a la* Attis), and mourned over until his resurrection.

As Caesar had been murdered as a result of a conspiracy of Senators and high officials, the Jesus play would eventually come to include such things as the bogus trial of Jesus by the Sanhedrin—the Judean institution that most closely approximated the Roman Senate. Like the plot to kill Caesar and the immediate aftermath of nocturnal political manoeuvrings, the Sanhedrin trial smacks of conspiracy as it is hurriedly convened and held at night, with agents rushing out to search for (false) witnesses in the dark. In Mark's gospel, no names of the Jewish high priests are given—a further clue that the trial is thematic and theatrical rather than historical. It is only the later gospels that provide the names of Caiaphas and Annas as high priests in Jerusalem. More historical grist is demanded of the cult as time goes by. But it is still all centred around his death, not his life—as should be expected of something developing from a commemoration.

The costly anointing of Christ (Mk 14) and the disciples' protest against it make sense theatrically, i.e.—they respectively symbolise and illustrate the arrogance of the pretender Jesus. The gospels present this as the trigger for Judas to execute his betrayal (Jn 12:4–5). It was precisely the perceived arrogance of Caesar and the republican fear that he was setting himself up as king that sealed his fate.

Beware the Ides of Nisan

I earlier highlighted the absurdity in Mark telling us (Mk 14:2) that the chief priests did not want to seize Jesus on the sacred feast day "lest there be an uproar of the people" when he himself tells us that they wound up crucifying him on that very day in full public view. But it is true that Caesar's assassins needed to murder him at the Ides Senate meeting as he would be away from the saluting crowds, and he was to leave Rome just four days later on his campaign against the Parthians. The gospel writers have sought to capture the urgency of the Caesar assassination. But it was the *Ides of March conspirators who had to move quickly*—the gospels don't provide a credible reason for why the Ides of Nisan conspirators needed to.

To entice Caesar to the Senate meeting Decimus Brutus told him that the Senators would proclaim him king of the Roman provinces. So how appropriate that the first question to Christ put into the mouth of Pilate, "governor" of the Roman province of Judea, is—

"Art thou the king of the Jews?"

For, although they might have squabbled over *who* should be their king, the Jews had no qualms about having one *per se*. The dread of kings was a Roman obsession, aptly captured in the seduction of Brutus by Shakespeare's Cassius—

> "Now in the name of all the gods at once, upon what meat doth this our Caesar feed that he is grown so great?...when could they say till now who talked of Rome that her wide walls encompassed but one man?...O, you and I have heard our fathers say there was a Brutus once that would have brooked the Eternal Devil to keep his state in Rome as easily as a King!"

So the devil who "entered" Judas was Cassius Longinus who persuaded Brutus to perform his infamous act. Small wonder that these three men dangle from the mouths of the hideous Satan in the pit of *Dante's Inferno*. The "sword of Longinus" even survives in Christian apocryphal tradition and populist literature as the sword that killed Christ.

The ostensibly reverential supplications that the Ides conspirators first made to Caesar on bended knee were a mockery. They then tore the purple robe from the shoulder of the unarmed man. This would have been seen as a monstrous indignity by his supporters, and has been immortalised in the gospels wherein Jesus is dressed in a regal purple robe, then stripped, buffeted and mocked prior to being executed. Luke has Herod's men doing this (for obvious propagandistic reasons), but the other gospels still portray it as being performed by Roman soldiers.

The Jesus tragedy, in short, is a crystallisation of the essential elements of Caesar's fate under a Judaic guise, and grafted onto the coincidental calendar of the Attis dying/resurrecting god ritual. Evidence that "Jesus Christ" may have grown out of a religious play of sorts even lies in one of Paul's letters. As I will shortly demonstrate, Paul gives us virtually no details of the *life* of the gospel Jesus, but, as J M Robertson noted, he wrote—

> "O foolish Galatians, who hath bewitched you, that you should not obey the truth, before whose eyes Jesus Christ hath been evidently set forth, crucified among you?" (Gal 2:1)

What on earth did Paul mean by this? How could Jesus, who the gospels tell us died in Jerusalem, have been crucified in Galatia? Does this mean that Jesus was even then being impersonated by the lead player in an *Oberammergau* style Passion play? Or does it mean that Paul was apprised of the information that there had been a large contingent of Galatians tourists in Jerusalem for Christ's fatal Passover? Phrygia, in Galatia, is the original domicile of Attis. Now it is time to look at exactly what Paul understood by the "Jesus Christ" that he preached.

The Enigma of Paul

For the Jews require a sign and the Greeks seek after wisdom
—but we preach Christ crucified!—St Paul

The proof that there was no "Jesus of Nazareth" lies in the writings of Paul, who the book of Acts tells us came from Tarsus. Who was this man? What was his understanding of "Jesus Christ", and what did he mean by these words he wrote to the Christians at Corinth? The purpose of this chapter is to demonstrate that the above quote epitomises Paul's picture of Jesus Christ. I shall further argue that Paul never thought that any of his contemporaries ever knew Jesus Christ personally, nor did he think that anybody should have. This is borne out by a careful reading of his epistle to the Galatians. But first a quick overview of Paul and his letters.

Paul was recognized as an *apostle,* as is affirmed by such later writers as Clement of Rome. An apostle (*apostolos—messenger*) in early Christian understanding is a messenger spiritually commissioned by God—not to be confused with a *disciple,* which means a follower or student (*matthetes—from which derives mathematics*) and can imply a personal relationship with the teacher. Paul is the author of the earliest Christian documents we know of, and he is the only apostle that we have any writings from at all. It is widely agreed that he is the principal author of *Romans, 1 & 2 Corinthians, 1 Thessalonians, Galatians, Philippians, Colossians,* and *Philemon. Ephesians* and *2 Thessalonians* carry the imprint of his thinking but have been subjected to various modifications and embellishments. *1 & 2 Timothy* and *Titus* attempt to borrow his authority, but unconvincingly, and are known as the "pseudo-Paulines" or "Pastorals"—they hail from the 2nd century. The mystical epistle to the Hebrews was not originally, and is no longer, ascribed to him.

The importance of Paul's own letters is that they were written between about 50 to 60 AD, some time *after* Paul's meetings with the various apostles in Jerusalem whom tradition holds were associates and disciples of "Jesus of Nazareth". Of course, Paul's letters were written long before the canonical gospels and the book of Acts which bear this tradition. But what is astounding about his letters is that they seem to indicate that he had virtually no awareness of the pre-crucifixion life of Jesus, and no knowledge of the details of that crucifixion. Moreover, he does not even use the word "crucifixion" in the historical or substantive sense, but rather employs more adjectival forms like "Christ crucified" or "Christ, who was crucified". All this is in keeping with his proclamation "we *preach* Christ crucified".

Now there are a few pieces of text within Paul's writings that suggest he had some idea of the circumstances of the death of Jesus that could, with some difficulty, be reconciled with our gospels. I will deal with these at the end of this chapter so they can be viewed in context. Here I want to look at the general tone of his letters, and what specific parts of them—especially Galatians—mean for the historicity of Jesus of Nazareth.

Significantly, Paul never uses the word "disciple", *even when referring to the members of the Jerusalem sect of the Christian cult.* He says nothing about the life of Jesus, he never mentions his miracles or exorcisms and does not quote a single one of his teachings. He rather tortures the ancient Hebrew scriptures to back his multitudinous admonitions, passing over far more apt quotes from the gospel Jesus. Although he repeatedly asserts that Christ rose from the dead, he never says anything about the timing, the venue, or the political drama involved. He never refers to John the Baptist, Jesus' now famous sermons, the Pharisees who plotted Jesus' murder, the noble Nicodemus, the perfidious Sanhedrin trial under Caiaphas, Pilate, the various Marys, Judas nor any other persons or events significant or insignificant in Jesus' career.

Why is this so? Those who think that Jesus existed—the historicists—sometimes answer this by arguing that Paul found no occasion to mention these details about Jesus, or, worse still, that he did not want to mention them because they conflicted with his "agenda". There are many criticisms that could be made of this, but suffice it to say at the outset that Paul would have needed to acquaint himself with as much knowledge of the real Jesus as possible because, if the gospels are anything to go by, he would have been asked many questions in his peregrinations about Jesus' cryptic sayings and deeds by some of the multitudinous thousands who actually had met him—I stress, going by the gospels, that is.

This silence by Paul about the career of Jesus the man is even more remarkable when we consider how close Paul was to the time Jesus allegedly lived and to the men Jesus supposedly knew. In his letter to the Galatians, Paul claims that God revealed "his son" to him in a supernatural vision. He vehemently asserts that he learned *nothing* about Christ from any human being—

> "…but I certify you, brethren, that the gospel that was
> preached of me is not after man, for I neither received it of

man, neither was I taught it, but by the revelation of Jesus Christ" (Gal 1:11, 12)

Before trying to learn anything about the deity Jesus Christ from people who already professed a belief in him, Paul went to Arabia and returned to Damascus (v 17). We can infer from this that he probably had his original vision from God while he was *in* Damascus, not on the road to it. When the Damascan governor under King Aretas tried to arrest him—for what reason is not stated—he escaped by being lowered from the city walls in a basket (2 Cor 11:32, 33). This is when he chose to go to Jerusalem—

> "Then after three years I went up to Jerusalem to see Peter, and abode with him fifteen days. But other of the apostles saw I none, save James the Lord's brother. Now the things that I write unto you, behold, *before God*, I lie not." (KJV, Gal 1:18–20)

[Here I should point out that many people believe that "the Lord's brother" was Jesus' sibling. The Greek—*ton adelphon tou kuriou*—transliterates as "the brother of the Lord". The more familiar sounding "the Lord's brother" is a peculiarity of English. I shall return to this belief.] So, what year was it when Paul met these men in Jerusalem? Paul's first trip there, by his own account, was three years after his original celestial vision from God. King Aretas died in 40 AD, so the latest that Paul could have gone to Jerusalem to meet those men is 43 AD. Pontius Pilate was the Prefect of Judea from 26 to 36 AD. If Jesus Christ was crucified at the beginning of Pilate's prefecture, the earliest Paul's Jerusalem trip could have been is 29 AD. The minimum gap between Jesus' death and Paul's trip must be three years, and the maximum is seventeen years. This gives us a mean of ten years; Paul should have been able to avail himself of just about as much inside information about Jesus as he wanted.

But the explicit point that Paul makes to the Galatians is that he learnt nothing about Christ from any human agencies, and that he was preaching him long before meeting any other apostles; and that therefore his preaching—what he calls his "gospel"—came by direct celestial inspiration. We can further infer that these two particular apostles in Jerusalem, Peter and James, did not know Jesus and were relative lightweights—otherwise Paul's angry oath makes no sense. He would be saying in essence "How could I have learned anything about Jesus when I was up in Jerusalem? I only spoke to Peter, his personally deputised first priest, and James, his sibling brother—I swear to God!" It is crucially important to recognise that Paul is not saying that he preached his own celestially revealed gospel *until* he met Peter and James, but also thereafter—as the sequel indicates. For the next eleven years he went about preaching in Syria and Cilicia—

> "Then after fourteen years I went up again to Jerusalem and communicated unto them that gospel that I preach amongst the gentiles, but privately to them that were of reputation, lest by any means I should run, or had run, in vain." (Gal 2:1, 2)

He obviously had not been running in vain; otherwise he would have needed to amend his gospel, which he tells us he did not. But what does he mean by "them that were of reputation"? The historicists take this to mean men who knew Jesus personally. But if that is the case, why didn't Paul just say so? Why should he choose to be so cryptic? Why did he not just say "then I communicated privately with men who actually had known Jesus"? The historicists must also explain their opinion of the status of Peter. If being "of reputation" means knowing Jesus personally, Paul had already, in the terms of the historicist case, spoken to such a person—Peter—on his first visit to Jerusalem. As noted, the historicists also usually claim that the "James" in Jerusalem that Paul met all those years before was Jesus' sibling brother, which induces them to think that Jesus existed, as phantoms don't have siblings. If they were right, it would mean that being formed in the same womb as the co-creator of the universe—Paul's own understanding of Jesus Christ (see his descriptions—e.g. Colossians 1:15–20 & Philippians 2:5–11)—and also being an *apostle* of that co-creator, did not qualify the hapless James to be regarded as a "man of reputation". The historicists are constrained by their own beliefs to admit that Paul's use of the term "of reputation" does not imply knowing Jesus personally.

Is it not more likely that "the brother of the Lord" was a title honouring Jerusalem James' piety or charity, in the same way that we today have such orders as "the little sisters of Jesus"? And is it not also likely that the phrase "them that were of reputation" here implies others' opinions of the character or abilities of the men in question—rather than whether they knew someone, in this case Jesus, or not?

But let's again assume that the historicists are right, i.e. that these men in Jerusalem knew Jesus the man. Paul tells us that alongside these men "of reputation" were "false brethren"—false, that is, because they were rather concerned about adhering to traditional Mosaic customs, and they saw Paul as a crypto-antinomian. Further on, he tells us that these men who "seemed to be somewhat...*added nothing unto me*" (Gal 2:4, 6). He is not implying here that these men *refused* to tell him all about Jesus, rather that they did tell him everything they knew, and that what they knew was nothing more than what he already knew himself. Paul, who appears to have hailed from Damascus (or Tarsus), who never knew Jesus (as the historicist would agree) and apparently had never been in Jerusalem before his visit some years after his heavenly revelation (he was "unknown" to them by face—Gal 1:22), could learn *nothing* about Jesus from Jesus' friends, associates and relatives. Does this mean that they could not tell him anything about his personal demeanour, habits, manner of speaking, opinions, sense of humour, length of hair, colour of eyes, attitude to women, attitude to authority etc? It is quite obvious that they could not tell him anything about Jesus' attitude to the Mosaic Law, because if these men had been taught and instructed by their friend and associate Jesus, their view of the Mosaic Law should have been in line with his—otherwise why would they have been his followers?

If these men in Jerusalem were intimates and followers of the highly opinionated *preacher* Jesus whom the historicists think Paul was claiming to represent, why, in their dispute with Paul, did they not just say "Listen Paul, these are Jesus' opinions, not ours. We're dreadfully sorry, but you never knew him". Further to this, if Paul thought these "false brethren" were ignoring or abrogating a teaching of their dearly departed master Jesus, would he not say so? We must not loose sight of the fact that the burning issue in the Galatian epistle is the matter of whether circumcision—apparently literal and metonymous—should be insisted upon for local converts (it obviously would not have been a major issue in, for example, Hispania). So were Jesus and his sibling brother circumcised, or not? There are no halfway positions here—one cannot be half circumcised—and the men who dedicated their lives to following Jesus should have known exactly what his status was. So why did the Jerusalem apostles not defend themselves against Paul with their advantageous personal knowledge of Jesus?

And what about the people that Paul was writing to? Did the Galatians also believe that these men in Jerusalem had shared Jesus' life and that Paul could learn nothing from them? If so, the Galatians must have thought Jesus a taciturn character indeed. But today, for reason's sake, we must admit that—even if Jesus had been a deaf mute—men who actually knew him would obviously be able to tell Paul personal things about him that Paul could not have known.

The historicists have never furnished a satisfactory explanation for this problem. The mythicist case is frequently met with disdain by people who really have no idea how problematic Jesus' historicity is. Christian apologists often deceive the believers by misrepresenting the mythicist case. This is achieved by only responding to the most extreme and aberrant arguments—usually the discredited ones of the early French atheist school—and then closing the book on the case. I think it was Arthur Drews who reasoned that if there had been a man called Jesus who was the first cause of Christianity, the men who knew him would have needed to be completely overwhelmed by his personality and charisma to have elevated him to the status of Lord and creator of the universe almost immediately upon his death. Having held him in such high esteem, they must have waited on his every utterance with bated breath, watched his every action and movement in the hope that perhaps they might emulate him. Yet the only letter we have that deals with Paul's meeting with these apostles in Jerusalem by the names of James, Peter, and John evinces no personal impact on these men by Jesus at all. This question still demands an answer: why could Paul learn nothing about Jesus from the apostles in Jerusalem?

Paul refers to James, Cephas—presumed to be Peter—and John as men who "*seemed* to be pillars" because they accepted his divinely appointed apostleship as long as he would give them money (for the poor) and because they seemed to be happy enough with his non-insistence on circumcision for gentile converts (Gal 2:7–10). Many orthodox Jerusalem Jews (and apparently Christians) thought that it was unclean to dine with the *ethnon*—ethnics, i.e. non-Jews. Peter had apparently been happy to dine with Paul alongside "gentiles" up in Antioch until a party of men were sent there by Jerusalem James, which induced Peter to withdraw from their company (v 12). Paul claims he assailed Peter in front of others with the devastating question—"if you, being a Jew, live after the manner of gentiles, and not as the Jews do, why do you compel the gentiles to live as the Jews?" (v 14) This would appear to be the bottom line. Paul tells the Galatians that he told Peter that the Mosaic laws did not have to be obeyed because *they are really just impractical.* Many people might perhaps agree with him, but doesn't Christianity generally teach that Jesus' teachings, and expiating *crucifixion*, did away with the need to observe those Mosaic laws?

Did Jesus himself know anything about this? If so, why did he never mention it to Peter? If Peter's life was dramatically changed by his personal association with Jesus, what could it have been about Jesus that impressed him? It could scarcely have been that Jesus taught him that the Mosaic Law was to be superseded, because Paul would not have had to bring him around to that point of view. It can hardly be the case that Jesus was an inspiring traditionalist either, because one single quote by Peter from a conservative Jesus on the matter would have stumped Paul. And Paul does not regard Peter as an apostate—he gives no indication that he thinks that Peter is contravening an *edict* of Jesus. Rather, he upbraids him for contravening common sense.

[Paul, further on his letter when waxing theological, describes the Mosaic Law as a kind of curse—a curse because the smallest infraction of it is punishable by death whilst the observing of it is all but impossible. He then declares "Christ hath redeemed us from the curse of the law, being made a curse for us—for it is written 'Cursed is he that hangeth from a tree'" (Gal 3:13). The Jerusalem apostles could hardly have been promoting this message, they appear to have been blissfully unaware of it. Nevertheless, Paul himself, when the chips were really down, revealed the true reason for his quasi-antinomian preaching. He thought the Jewish laws were too punctilious. Christ's selfless sin-expiating sacrifice is only the second line of defence!]

So it is clear that Paul does not refute Peter by reminding him of any teaching of Jesus, and vice versa, but neither of the two seem to have called upon Jesus as an exemplar either. This is the only other way that Jesus could have taught—by example, like Gandhi. In fact he should have been the exemplar *par excellence*. Consider the gospel stories of Jesus associating with publicans (the hated tax collectors) and sinners, and his defending himself against the Pharisees for doing so (e.g. Mk 2:15–17). This behaviour on the part of Jesus is akin to Paul dining with the uncircumcised, an act that offended Peter when the Mosaic traditionalists were present. Was Peter aware of Jesus' downgrading of the need to observe strict Mosaic customs when he—pointedly right in front of the religious authorities—picked corn on the Sabbath (Mk 2:23–27), healed on the Sabbath (see Mk 3:1–6) etc? In fact, Mark portrays these liberal views of, or abrogation of, the Mosaic Law by Jesus as the very reason why the Pharisees first sought to kill him (v 6)! These radically progressive actions of Jesus offended their unreconstructed conservatism. Were the reasons for why Jesus was ultimately executed so unimportant to Paul and Peter? Peter, in the gospels, is present for all these above occasions wherein Jesus repudiates a strict interpretation of the Mosaic Law—and Paul has to go to so much effort to persuade *him* that he thinks the Mosaic Law is impractical? Something here does not add up.

Paul appears to have successfully won his debate with Peter, and I suggest that the reason for this is very simple. Peter, and the other apostles in Jerusalem, could not tell Paul any of these stories about Jesus because their preaching and beliefs were not based on knowing any such person, and the earthly biography of "Jesus Christ" that we today are familiar with had not been written yet. So the whole notion that Jesus was put to death by political and social reactionaries must be a fiction, otherwise he could hardly be the founder of such a conservative and traditional sect as the Jerusalem branch appears to have been.

Not only did the apostles in Jerusalem not know Jesus personally, they do not even seem to have had any second-hand information on him. If we allow that Jesus had been so dull as not to even have an opinion on circumcision—clearly a major issue to everyone else concerned—why didn't the Jerusalem apostles just use a ruse? If it were widely known to the Christian community that these men knew and were taught by Jesus—which is the usual reason the historicists proffer for why Paul never mentions it—why didn't they just *pretend* that Jesus had a conservative view on circumcision? It really would have been that easy.

There are even greater problems for the historicists if those Jerusalem apostles were associates of Jesus. Whatever became of the momentous political drama the gospels describe of his death? No one seems to have attached any significance to the fact that Paul had no problems *finding* the Jerusalem apostles. There is no indication that he had to sneak into the city and furtively enquire as to the whereabouts of the friends and supporters of the man who had only recently been crucified as a felon. In the gospels the Jewish authorities go to incredible lengths to ensure that they eliminate Jesus—procuring false witnesses, hiring a betrayer, hurriedly convening a nocturnal kangaroo court, stirring up unseemly elements in a mob to crucify Jesus merely for his claiming to be the son of God—a claim they could have dismissed as the delusions of a madman. Yet apparently within no time at all, the proto-Christian church is snugly ensconced in Jerusalem and no early writers remark on the irony. It is quite clear from Paul's letter to the Galatians that the Jerusalem church was the headquarters of that region. So, move heaven and earth to execute one man who could simply be written off as a lunatic, yet allow the local church to set up shop and openly preach that *the existing authorities just killed the Son of God!*

It will not do for the historicists to argue that the Jerusalem church would not be doing just that. If they are prepared to dismiss the gospel accounts of the Jewish and Roman authorities supervising the crucifixion (along with the attendant mob scenes), they have to provide alternative culprits. An event can hardly be regarded as historical if none of the players in the only records we have of it were involved. As I say, if Jesus was crucified late in Pilate's prefecture, Paul's trip to Jerusalem can only be a maximum of about seven years after the event. Most of the authorities, especially the Sanhedrin who we are told engineered Jesus' death, would still be in office. If not, the current officials would mostly be the immediate successors of them. If we excuse Paul's lack of curiosity about Jesus' activities by positing that Jesus was crucified early in Pilate's career, we still have to confront the absurdity that the Jerusalem church—which obviously existed for some time before Paul (by his own admission) came on the scene—had been teaching that the governor, who just works across the road at the Praetorium, recently killed the Son of God. Not only that, but almost all the contemporary ruling Jewish authorities were complicit in the deicide. Why would Pilate and the Sanhedrin not just pounce on anyone making such accusations and dispatch them? (Pilate would not have hesitated to do just that—see *Problems with Passion Week* in this book). Where is the evidence of the aftermath of such events described in the book of Acts as Peter accusing the assembled authorities—point blank—of deicide (see Acts 4:5–11)?

The questions do not end here. Why does Paul show no interest in meeting people who were close to Jesus? Would he not at least want to meet Mary, the woman who gave birth to the demigod he was claiming created the universe? Did he have no interest in meeting the earnest Nicodemus, to whom Jesus revealed the secret that we must be "born again"? Or what about the saintly Joseph of Arimathea, who generously donated the tomb which provided the venue for the greatest event in all of Paul's universe—Christ's ground-breaking resurrection from the dead—the very centrepiece of his preaching? Would he not yearn to visit the vacant tomb itself? Or the hallowed site of Calvary? While in Jerusalem, would he not hunger to reverently enter the chamber of the Last Supper, where his God had only recently instituted the Eucharist? Mark told us—

> "And the first day of unleavened bread, when they killed the Passover, his disciples said unto him (Jesus), Where wilt thou that we go and prepare that thou mayest eat the Passover? And he sendeth forth two of his disciples, and saith unto them, Go ye into the city, and there shall meet you a man bearing a pitcher of water: follow him. And wheresoever he shall go in, say ye to the good man of the house, The Master saith, Where is the guest chamber, where I shall eat the Passover with my disciples? And he will shew you a large upper room furnished and prepared: there make ready for us. And his disciples went forth, and came into the city, and found as he had said unto them: and they made ready the Passover." (Mk 14:12–16)

Peter, or the other disciples who found the room and prepared the fateful repast, could presumably have used their good offices with the "good man" to take Paul right to the very chair that Jesus had sat upon. Was it not just yesterday? And on the subject of chairs, why did Paul show no interest in Jesus' handiwork as a carpenter while he was in town? We know that Paul was preaching Jesus Christ as the co-creator of the universe, would he show no interest in seeing something that Jesus had created on earth—a chair, a table, a lamp-stand? Such items should have been of inestimable value to Paul, and he should have had as much access to them as he wanted. And he cannot be excused by our positing that he was not into curios—some of these items could have been, at the very least, auctioned off at church fairs to raise money for the poor. Of course there are some who would argue that Mark was only using a clever metaphor when he had Jesus' townspeople refer to him as a carpenter—a view which hardly undermines my general thesis here!

Such questions as those posed above are never answered. It is customarily assumed that Paul went to Jerusalem to find out more about Jesus from men who actually knew him (the book of Acts pretends this), even though Paul does not say this in his Galatian letter—nor anywhere else for that matter. If Paul thought that these apostles in Jerusalem personally knew the very deity whom he was preaching, why did he wait so long before going to see them, and Jesus' other intimates? Had Jesus been a great mathematician, there would have been no pressing need to speak to his contemporaries. All his important work would have been committed to paper, and his friends and relatives would only have been able to furnish the curious with little more than sentimental reminiscences of his lifestyle and habits. But Paul is preaching a *demigod*, one who the gospels tell us had a mighty preaching career. Barring being possessed of the privilege of direct revelation, word of mouth was the only means by which one could learn about his teachings after his demise. Common sense would insist that it should have been a priority for Paul to speak to as many people as possible about the recently deceased Jesus while their memories were fresh, even if only to ensure that he was not blatantly contradicting one of his edicts.

Paul actually only refers to the Jerusalem leaders as "those who were *apostles* before me", and never mentions them as having been disciples of Jesus. Here I must illustrate a tactic of NT propaganda. Mark only uses the word *apostles* once, when Jesus sends his disciples on a specific mission to proclaim his message (see Mk 6:7–13; 6:30—the text is interrupted by a pericope about Herod's execution of John the Baptist). When they return from that mission Mark refers to them as *apostles*, in the same manner that a teacher who had certain students might refer to them as *competitors* if they had just taken part in a foot race. But Luke uses the term six times. He specifically refers to Jesus' twelve disciples as apostles—"And when it was day, he called unto him his disciples: and of them he chose twelve, whom also he named apostles" (Lk 6:13). He then uses the word in five other places, including the Last Supper and resurrection scenes where Mark exclusively employs the term disciples. Luke's most intrepid usage of it is where he has adapted the source that Matthew also had access to. Matthew has Jesus complain to his contemporaries—

> "Wherefore, behold, I send unto you *prophets and wise men and scribes*: and some of them ye shall kill and crucify; and some of them shall ye scourge in your synagogues, and persecute them from city to city: That upon you may come all the righteous blood shed upon the earth, from the blood of righteous Abel unto the blood of Zacharias son of Barachias, whom ye slew between the temple and the altar. (Matt 23:34–35)

As we shall see in chapter eight, Jesus posits himself here as the Jewish God, using OT terminology to condemn the Pharisees for a political killing which took place shortly before the onset of the Roman/Jewish war as described by Josephus. But Luke's version is quite different—

> "Therefore also said the wisdom of God, *I will send them prophets and apostles*, and some of them they shall slay and persecute: That the blood of all the prophets, which was shed from the foundation of the world, may be required of this generation; From the blood of Abel unto the blood of Zacharias, which perished between the altar and the temple." (Lk 11:49–51)

Luke here is propagating notions that are consistent with the tradition that such apostles as Peter and Paul suffered persecution. He has "christianised" Jesus' essentially Jewish historical lament. In both his gospel and the book of Acts he blurs the distinction between disciples and apostles—subtly melding them into one and the same thing—to actively promote the perception that the apostles in Jerusalem were personal associates of Jesus Christ.

However, Paul's Galatian reference to his own and Peter's commissioning by God makes them sound as if they were of the same nature and status (see Gal 2:8—the Greek uses a different form of the same verb to describe both), which means that it must have been generally understood that Peter "knew" Jesus in the same way that Paul did—by direct celestial revelation. He was a man with a message from God, an apostle. Peter and Paul "knew" Jesus in the same fashion that Glen Campbell "knew" Jesus before he was a Superstar.

Paul's knowledge of Jesus' biography seems to be little more than an extrapolation on the SS texts in Isaiah 52:13–53:12 (All the early Christian writers seem to have had a similar view). Apart from this, he seems to have thought that Jesus had been crucified somewhere in the indeterminate past, that he was a "son of

David' (Rom 1:3—this, of course, was a messianic expectation) and was "made of a woman" (Gal 4:4). These scanty points sound theological rather than historical, as Paul's teaching is exclusively centred on the religious *meaning* of the death and resurrection of "Jesus Christ"—

> "For I determined not to know anything among you, save Jesus Christ, and him crucified." (1 Cor 2:2)

Paul does not mean by this that he chose not to learn anything about Jesus' activities, he is rather stressing that promoting faith in Jesus Christ is his mission in life. If the belief that Christ had lived and died came from liturgical readings of the SS texts around Passover gradually being taken as an inspired record of real events, we should expect his historical time setting to be expressed in vague terms in the earliest writings. Paul obliges admirably—

> "When the fullness of time was come, God sent forth his son, made of a woman, made under the law, to redeem them that were under the law, that we might receive the adoption of sons." (Gal 4:4, 5)

And elsewhere—

> "For when we were yet without strength, Christ died for the ungodly." (Rom 5:6)

These are the only temporal references Paul makes to Jesus' existence. Just how this relates to earthly time in Paul's idiosyncratic Weltanschauung, is shrouded in mystery. He seems to be saying that, whenever it occurred, it was at precisely the right time for God's arcane soteriological purposes—rather the ring of a mystic credo, venue and time unspecified, than a description of a near contemporary event. One would expect him to have written something like "last year", or "four years ago", or even "recently". Indeed the exact *date and time* should have been sacred to him. He does think that it occurred on Passover, "For even Christ our Passover is sacrificed for us" (1 Cor 5:7), but that is not helpful, as the sacrifice of the "Passover lamb" occurs every year, and has since time immemorial.

Note also Paul's impersonal reference to Jesus being "made of a woman". This epistle was written after he had met the apostles in Jerusalem *twice*, and Mary should still have been alive at this period. Even if he had no time to meet Mary, why did he not add something like "…made of a woman, who, as you all know, is called Mary, and a very fine woman she is too", or perhaps some other endearing reference? Alternatively, if she were deceased, "…made of a woman, the beloved Mary, who sadly left us recently and is in the bosom of Christ" etc. Would one really need to be reminded that someone who was unquestionably a real man had been "made of a woman"?

All of this is consistent with the quote from Paul at the head of this chapter. It was the Jews who generally believed that a Christ figure should perform signs and wonders, and the Greeks thought that a Christ figure should be a wise and righteousness teacher (the later gospel writers generously filled in these blanks). "*But…*", says Paul, "…*we* preach Christ *crucified*". I hope it is not facile to point out that if it were well known that Jesus had been crucified it would not be necessary to preach it. Paul should have been saying, "We preach that Jesus (of Nazareth, or some other identifying tag; whom you all know was publicly crucified etc) was the Christ". (And in fact, the later book of Acts, sensibly enough, makes Paul do just this. He, and his colleagues, disciples and proxies, repeatedly argue that *Jesus of Nazareth* was the Christ! See e.g. Acts 18.) For Paul himself, the theological definition maketh the man, the attributes of the man proper are never referred to the definition.

To sum up, if Jesus Christ in Paul's time was an abstract deity whom nobody, including all the original apostles, knew personally, then Paul's letter to the Galatians is intelligible. On the other hand, if the apostles in Jerusalem were intimates of Jesus then the letter is an affront to common sense.

Now it might be apparent to the reader why I have left the few texts in Paul's letters that indicate he may have known something about the earthly Jesus, which loosely accords with the gospels, to the end of this chapter. Without being aware of the above arguments it would be all too easy to think that my objections to the following texts are unreasonable. Consider this familiar piece in Paul's first Corinthian epistle—

> "For I have received it of the Lord that which I also delivered unto you, That the Lord Jesus the same night in which he was *betrayed* took bread; and when he had given thanks, he brake it, and said; Take, eat; this is my body, which is broken for you—do this in remembrance of me." (1 Cor 11:23–41 KJV)

The word translated "betrayed" here is rendered as "delivered" or "handed over" in the Greek, and is a different form of the same verb used in the Septuagint in reference to Isaiah's SS, who was "delivered to death" The implication here, as all good Christian exegetes know, is sacrificial. The beneficent SS, who substitutes for the sacrificial Passover lamb, selflessly hands himself over "unto God" for the benefit of the inveterate sinners. But because Judas "delivers" Jesus into the hands of the Sanhedrin posse, the King James translators have allowed their acquaintance with the traditional gospels to influence their rendition. Some translations even interpolate the name "Judas".

There is no dispute that this letter was written after Paul's two trips to Jerusalem. If Paul wrote the above text "I have received it of the Lord", we have to assume that Peter also forgot, or chose not, to tell Paul about the inauguration of the Lord's Supper, at which the gospels tell us he was present. Again this raises the question of what these two men spent their time talking about. Another possibility is that Paul, in order to raise his own status, chose not to reveal that he gleaned the information from Peter. But for this to be true, Paul would have needed to be confident that the Corinthians weren't familiar with (what we know as) the standard Last Supper story either, otherwise he would have been seriously jeopardising his credibility by not citing Peter as his source. To really prove the case, he should have written something (in essence) like—

> "Peter told me that Jesus took bread at the Last Supper and
> said 'Eat this in remembrance of me.' And Peter should know,
> because he was there."

Paul declared that he learnt nothing about Jesus in Jerusalem. So, if Peter was not at the Last Supper, just who was? However, Paul may not have written this Corinthian piece. From verse 20 he seems to be complaining about parishioners "pigging out" at church meals, and he suggests that they should eat and drink at home. If we omit the material dealing with the Lord's Supper, verses 23–32, we have—

> "When ye come together into one place, this is not to eat the
> Lord's Supper. For in eating everyone taketh before another his
> own supper—and one is hungry, and another is drunken.
> What? Have ye not houses to eat and to drink in? Or despise ye
> the church of God, and shame them that have not? What shall
> I say to you? Shall I praise you in this? I praise you not. (above
> text omitted here) Wherefore, my brethren, when ye come
> together to eat, tarry one for another. And if any man hunger,
> let him eat at home…"

The point of his letter is that church meals should be dignified, so anyone who is actually hungry should fill up before they go there. It might be that the doctrinal material about the Lord's Supper was added to Paul's letter later, but before the tradition of the Jerusalem Peter knowing an earthly Jesus had been developed. And on the other hand, if the text is authentic it again means that Paul's source is direct revelation, not hearsay from someone who had allegedly been there. Having the Lord Jesus institute the traditional supper is the best way to dignify it. Note that Paul does not specify to whom Jesus spoke these words. If "eye-witness" testimony is important, why did he not reveal who the witnesses were so the Corinthians could be assured that it was authentic? The idea that Jesus spoke these words to no one in particular is consistent with many of the inaugural activities of the ancient gods, who are quite frequently found to be talking to themselves ("Let there be light!" etc).

The second passage that needs to be looked at is where Paul is seeking to assure his readers that Christ rose from the dead—

> "Moreover, brethren, I declare unto you the gospel which I preached unto you, which also ye have received, and wherein ye stand; By which also ye are saved, if ye keep in memory what I preached unto you, unless ye have believed in vain. *For I delivered unto you first of all that which I also received, how that Christ died for our sins according to the scriptures; and that he was buried, and that he rose again the third day according to the scriptures. And that he was seen of Cephas, then of the twelve—After that, he was seen of above five hundred brethren at once; of whom the greater part remain unto this present, but some are fallen asleep.* After that, he was seen of James; then of all the apostles. And last of all he was seen of me also, as of one born out of due time. For I am the least of the apostles, that am not meet to be called an apostle, because I persecuted the church of God. But by the grace of God I am what I am—and his grace which was bestowed upon me was not in vain; but I laboured more abundantly than they all—yet not I, but the grace of God which was with me. Therefore whether it were I or they, so we preach, and so ye believed.
>
> Now if Christ be preached that he rose from the dead, how say some among you that there is no resurrection of the dead? But if there is no resurrection of the dead, then Christ is not risen. And if Christ be not risen, then is our preaching vain, and your faith is also vain. For if the dead rise not, then is not Christ

raised, and if Christ be not raised, your faith is vain; ye are yet in your sins." (1 Cor 15:1–14, 16, 17)

We may be allowed to ask at the outset why there were people in the Corinthian church who did not believe in resurrection. Note that the author is saying that resurrection must be a true phenomenon, otherwise it would not have been possible for Christ to rise (rather than vice versa)! The section I have italicised contains a reference to "the twelve" that contradicts the gospel stories, wherein Jesus only appears to "the eleven"—as the betrayer Judas has demised, yet the text we just dealt with has Paul telling us that he is aware that Jesus had been "betrayed". The chronology also disagrees with the gospels wherein Jesus is first seen by a woman or a group of women, and only later by "the eleven" disciples. The gospels do not mention the five hundred eyewitnesses, and tell us nothing of an appearance to a James who is not part of "the eleven".

George Wells has raised objection to the apparent humility on Paul's part in this Corinthian text—Paul's placing of himself at the foot of the list of those privileged enough to see the resurrected Christ—as being inconsistent with Paul's haughty attitude towards the Jerusalem sect leaders as witnessed in his letter to the Galatians. Judging by the tone of that epistle, Paul does not sound like the kind of man who would humbly refer to himself as "the least of the apostles" who doesn't even merit to be called one. In fact he implies the exact opposite. Unless there was another mystery group of individuals down in Jerusalem who were of higher religious status than the supposed (by us) associates of Jesus, Paul disparages those very apostles as "men who *seemed* to be somewhat" who "added nothing" to him.

But Paul says that he "received" this information, and, consistent with the terminology of his repeated proclamations, this can only mean by direct revelation. I will leave it to the reader to ponder how impressed Paul's addressees would be to hear that God had "revealed" to him that multitudes had seen the resurrected Christ before he did. Gods are supposed to reveal hidden wisdom, not common knowledge. The italicised piece in the Corinthian quote above would appear to have been glossed or interpolated, it links Paul to a temporal event (Christ's death and resurrection). It seems to be the work of a harmonist painting over the kind of schisms that Clement complained about (more on this later). If we remove it we are left with a continuity which does not call for a comparison of what he and somebody else preaches.

In the italicised section, Paul assures his readers that there was a multitude of witnesses to Jesus' resurrection. He subsequently writes "…now if Christ be *preached* that he rose from the dead, how say some among you that there is no resurrection of the dead?" If Paul had in fact written the piece about the 500 witnesses, he should have followed it with something more like "If so many, then, saw Christ rise, why do you yet not believe" etc. He rather invokes a general belief in resurrection—which appears to have been gaining in popularity at the time—to buttress his case that Christ could have risen from the dead. So at the time in question there were people without the church that believed in resurrection, and Christians within the church that did not. Here we see the motive for the later provision of multitudinous witnesses to the resurrection of Christ.

Had the gospel writers been aware of the above material, and regarded it as written by Paul, it would seem strange that they did not report the story of the 500 witnesses (even the author of Luke/Acts doesn't report it). Paul's letter is believed to have been written around 54 AD, and the material about Christ dying and resurrecting reads like a doctrinal statement. The text might be an interpolation from a time when Paul's letters already had some status in certain quarters, but before the gospel traditions had been fully developed.

Another very good ground for thinking that the text is an interpolation is furnished by the 12th chapter of the letter of Clement, a church leader in Rome who wrote his own epistle to the Corinthians late in the 1st century. We know that he had Paul's first letter to the Corinthians in front of him, as he refers to it specifically and his paraphrasing of the schisms in the church Paul complained about agrees with our received texts. Although he, like Paul, believes that Jesus rose from the dead, he substantiates the case that resurrection is possible by citing the story of how the mighty Phoenix rises from its ashes down in Egypt. He writes of how the priests are stunned to find, every time they search the records, that it is always precisely five hundred years since the great bird's last resurrection. One would think that citing Paul's reference to the five hundred witnesses to Christ's resurrection would have been more to the point than praising the exploits of a mythical fowl. And it should also be noted that, again, "Paul" provides no venues for these resurrection appearances.

There is a third highly contentious Pauline text. In his letter to the Thessalonians he refers to the Jews—

> "…who both killed the Lord Jesus, and their own prophets, and have persecuted us; and they please not God, and are contrary to all men—Forbidding us to speak to the gentiles that they might be saved, to fill up their sins always—*for the wrath is come upon them to the uttermost.*" (1 Thess 2:15-6)

Many critics object to the caustic nature of this description of the Jews as being out of kilter with the general tenor of Paul's writings. Compare this with Romans 11, where Paul deals *specifically* with the matter of whether God has cast away the Israelites, by which he means the Jews. After asserting that the Jews have *not* been rejected by God, the worst indictment he brings against them is a generic breast-beating one from Elijah, "Lord they have killed thy prophets", but he does not mention the killing of Jesus in the same breath as he does in the above quote (nor anywhere else for that matter). This comes hot on the heels of his discussing of the Jews, and his concept of Christ, at length in his preceding two chapters (see Romans 9 & 10). This first letter to the Thessalonians is thought to have been written around 50 AD, but the words about wrath having come upon the Jews sounds like a reference to the calamitous Roman/Jewish war of 66–73 AD, which occurred after Paul had disappeared from the scene. The piece is widely regarded as an interpolation as it reflects the 2nd century church notion that Jerusalem was destroyed as a punishment for its inhabitants having killed Jesus.

The interpolater seems to have used the mechanism of reiterating Paul's thanksgiving of 1 Thess 1:2–6 "and you became followers of us and of the Lord" after which he praises their exemplary effect on "all that believed in Macedonia and Achaia" (v 7). In the section in question, he introduces his accusation against "the Jews" by paraphrasing the earlier text thus "For you, brethren, became followers of the churches of God which in Judea are in Christ Jesus" (1 Thess 2:14). It might be remembered that Paul would be unlikely to hold the Judean Christians up as exemplars for the Thessalonians when he had experienced such acrimonious disputes with them about the Mosaic Law. However, introducing the churches of *Judea* here provided the hook to hang the slander on.

Shortly after this, *in the same letter*, Paul does even better than ask us to believe that Christ resurrected, he even asks us to believe that he died as well—

> "For if we believe that Jesus died and rose again, even so them
> also which sleep in Jesus will God bring with him." (1 Thess
> 4:14)

Accusing people of murder when it is an article of faith that the victim died is a strange thing to do. But the questioned text speaks of the killing of Jesus as if it were an established fact. We may observe that no one had to be petitioned to believe that John Kennedy really expired. The implication in the complaint of "Paul" is that it would have been nice if the Jews had not killed Jesus. But for authentic Paul, Jesus Christ dying and resurrecting is a "package deal" belief, *wonderful news* that has been affirmed to him and other apostles by God, not something to be lamented over as a squalid murder as implied by the contentious text. For an excellent theological argument that it is an anti-semitic interpolation, see "1 Thess 2:13–16. A Deutero-Pauline Interpolation", B A Pearson, *Harvard Theological Review* 64 (1971) p 79–94.

These dubious texts in the letters of Paul are the only ones from which we can construe that he knew any details about Jesus' life. Again, they are minimal and only concern his death and resurrection. The suspicion that they may be interpolations is heightened by another reference by him to the crucifixion (as it were) that sits rather uncomfortably with the gospel records. He claims to be privy to mysteries and hidden wisdom ordained prior to the foundation of the universe—

> "...which none of the princes of this world knew—for had they known it, they would not have crucified the Lord of Glory." (1 Cor 2:8)

Were the Judean Jews the "princes of this world"? We can infer from Ephesians 2:2 "the prince of the power of the air (Satan)" and 6:12 that these "princes of this world" are the immediate underlings of Beelzebub himself—high ranking evil spirits. The gospels have Jesus being executed under the auspices of Rome, and give no suggestion that the Jewish chief priests were in the thrall of Satan's legions. Luke and John do have Satan entering Judas, but the gospel Satan surely knew who Jesus was, otherwise what was the dramatic temptation in the wilderness all about? In that account, Satan knew exactly who Jesus was, but failed to destroy him because Jesus K.O.'d him in the third round (see Lk 4:1–13). And furthermore, throughout the synoptic gospel stories, the demons that Jesus exorcises all immediately recognise him as the Son of God. Were the evil spirits truly benighted, or was the wisdom of these gospels stories hidden from the mystery-master Paul? What Paul really means by his gloat is that God pulled a swifty on the demons, and tricked them into killing Christ—something they would not want to do as they would understand the ramifications—universal salvation for the humankind they are hell-bent on destroying. In Paul's thinking, God's engineering of the slaying of Jesus is a magnificent coup.

If Paul had actually been familiar with the story that the Roman Pontius Pilate authorised Jesus' crucifixion, how could he have written Romans 13:1–7,

wherein he portrays the temporal powers, obviously Roman, as the servants of
God—

> "Let every soul be subject unto the higher powers. For there is
> no power but of God—the powers that be are ordained of
> God. Whosoever, therefore, that resisteth that power, resisteth
> the ordinance of God—and they that resist shall receive to
> themselves damnation. For rulers are not a terror to good
> works, but to the evil. Wilt thou then not be afraid of the
> power? Do that which is good, and thou shalt have praise of
> the same—For he is the minister of God to thee for good. But
> if thou do that which is evil, be afraid, for he beareth not the
> sword in vain—for he is the minister of God, a revenger to exe-
> cute wrath upon him that doeth evil. Wherefore you must
> needs be subject, not only for wrath, but also for conscience
> sake. For this cause pay ye tribute also—for they are God's
> ministers, attending continually upon this very thing. Render
> therefore to all their dues—tribute to whom tribute is due; cus-
> tom to whom custom; honour to whom honour."

So Paul wrote that the Roman and Roman authorised temporal rulers (he
obviously can't mean the "princes of this world"!) are not a threat to the doers of
good works, but only to evildoers. Should he not have isolated the execution of
Jesus Christ under Pilate and Caiaphas as a notable exception—especially if he
really penned the murder accusation against the Jews we just looked at? And if
the people to whom Paul was writing knew or believed that Jesus had recently
been crucified under the banner of Roman authority, how could they possibly
accept that Rome had the heavenly seal of approval? However, if Paul was preaching that benighted evil spirits were responsible for the death of Christ in another
realm at an indeterminate time, there is no contradiction.

And this is completely consonant with the wording Paul uses in reference to
the *parousia*, which he originally expected would occur in his lifetime. Paul himself believed that there were many different levels of being and dimensions of
heaven, and even humbly claimed to have visited one where he heard "unspeak-
able" words (2 Cor 12:1–7). It is probable that he thought that Jesus had been
spirited up to one of these levels and murdered there by evil angels who mistook
his identity. He does not write as though he believes that Jesus had just spent a

lifetime on earth. Tellingly, he never refers to the "*second* coming" of Christ, it is always simply the "coming". Consider these samples—

> "For as in Adam all die, even so in Christ shall all be made alive. But every man in his own order: Christ the firstfruits, afterward they that are Christ's at his *coming*." (1 Cor 15:22–23)

Some claim that the "coming", *parousia*—which means appearance—is the appearance of Christ in the hearts of the believer. But it is obvious that Paul is referring to a future event—the believers will be resurrected when Jesus comes. He cannot appear in the hearts of the dead.

> "For what is our hope, or joy, or crown of rejoicing? Are you not even to be in the presence of our Lord Jesus Christ at his *coming*? (1 Thess 2:19)

> "And the Lord make you to increase and abound in love one toward another...to the end that he may stablish your hearts unblameable...at the *coming* of our Lord Jesus Christ..." (1 Thess 3:12–13)

> "For this we say unto you by the word of the Lord, that we which are alive and remain unto the *coming* of the Lord shall not prevent them which are asleep." (1 Thess 4:14)

> "And the very God of peace sanctify you wholly, and I pray God your whole spirit and body be preserved blameless unto the *coming* of our Lord Jesus Christ." (1 Thess 5:23)

It is a consistent picture. My point is, if Paul knew that Jesus had played out his illustrious career—as presented in the gospels—only a few years before his own preaching career, it would be more natural for him to variously use terms like "when Christ returns", or, "when Jesus comes back to us", or, "when he comes again" etc. Was Paul at all aware of Jesus' brilliant exploits? Consider his advice to the Corinthians—

> "Let a man so account of us, as of the ministers of God...but with me it is a very small thing that I should be judged by you...yea, I judge not my own self. For I know nothing by myself...but he that judgeth me is the Lord. Therefore judge nothing before the time, *until the Lord come, who both will*

bring to light the hidden things of darkness, and will make manifest the counsels of the hearts…" (1 Cor 4:1–5)

Be patient, says Paul, for when Christ *comes*, he will do these great and notable things. Yet Luke tells us that Jesus, just a few years prior to Paul's writing, launched his earthly career thus—

"And Jesus returned in the power of the spirit into Galilee, and there went out a fame of him through all the region round about, and he taught in their synagogues, being glorified of all. And he came to Nazareth where he had been brought up, and as his custom was, he went into the synagogue on the Sabbath day, and stood up for to read. And there was delivered unto him the book of the prophet Isaiah. And when he opened the book, he found the place where it was written, The spirit of the Lord is upon me, *because he hath anointed me to preach the gospel to the poor, he hath sent me to heal the broken hearted, to preach deliverance to the captives, and recovering of sight to the blind, to set at liberty them that are bruised, To preach the acceptable year of the Lord.* And he closed the book, and he gave it again to the minister and sat down. And the eyes of all them that were in the synagogue were fastened upon him, and he began to say unto them—*This day is this scripture fulfilled in your ears."* (Lk 4:14–21)

Paul asserts that the gospel he preaches is by direct revelation from a heavenly Christ, and he regards himself as privileged to have received it. But the gospels trumpet that Christ has already *spectacularly* done the very kinds of things that Paul is telling his flock will soon take place at his coming. Every Joe in the synagogues of Judea and the coasts thereof has already heard Jesus' own version of his gospel direct from his lips, plus witnessed his stunning miracles—the "signs" and the "wisdom" that Paul spurns. Ahem.

It should be clear by now that the biography of the gospel Jesus cannot be reconciled with Paul's letters. But there are other epistle writers in the New Testament, some bearing names that accord with those Paul mentions in his letters. So now we should look at what they, and the early church fathers, have to say about the life of Jesus Christ.

The Ghost of Galilee

I want to say at the outset of this chapter that searching for the historical Jesus is like chasing a rainbow. The radiant arch of colour can be seen from a distance, but the closer one approaches the more it recedes until it ultimately dissipates, leaving one grasping at thin air. Our chief source of information on Jesus, the New Testament, is not very helpful. For a start, it is not compiled chronologically. The gospel of Matthew, the "greatest story ever told", is positioned before that of Mark, from which it was drawn. All four gospels and the book of Acts appear before Paul's letters, which are of earlier date and indeed some are pseudonymous. Even Paul's genuine letters are not arranged chronologically but cascade down to us in order of decreasing length, and may have been subjected to some interpolation.

The two letters of "Peter" in the NT were not written by the Peter who supposedly chewed the fat around the campfire with Jesus. The Christian writers, like their Jewish predecessors, would backdate their writings by ascribing them to deceased or legendary heroes for various reasons. "Daniel", for instance, was backdated almost four centuries to disguise the fact that it was a contemporary attack on the Syrian Greek rule of the Jewish territories just prior to the revolt of the Maccabees circa 167 BC. Backdating can also prove divine inspiration of the work by the impressive fulfilment of prophecy concerning events which have already come to pass. A more important reason is to lend greater status to the material being presented by claiming authorship by a prestigious figure of yesteryear. A case in point is the Judeo/Christian work *The Testaments of the Twelve Patriarchs.* Placing teachings in the mouths of the legendary twelve forefathers of Israel invests them with far more authority than if they were known to be the work of some contemporary writer. In the second epistle of "Peter" we find this assurance—

> "For we have not followed cunningly devised fables, when we made known unto you the power and coming of the Lord Jesus Christ, but were eyewitnesses to his majesty." (2 Pet 1:16)

We have just seen that "we" could not have "made known" this to Paul. This particular letter appears to have been cunningly devised in the 2nd century. The author warns against "backsliders", and in his third chapter he clearly dowses the hope of an early appearance of "the Lord". The sober light of day has come. By a subtle shift of emphasis the "coming" now appears to have already taken place, and the believers are admonished to savour the time when the "day-star" rises in their hearts—rather than waiting on the appearance of Jesus in person. Anyone familiar with the genuine writings of Paul would be aware that his principal message is that "the Lord" is *coming very soon!*—"the night is far spent, the day is at hand". It was the very imminence, not the immanence, of the Lord's majestic appearance that gave impetus to Paul's proselytising. (Modern evangelists try to pretend otherwise, for obvious reasons.) Peter was a contemporary of Paul's and had he been telling everyone that the great day of the Lord's appearance was some time off (a *thousand years* is as a day! See 2 Pet 3:3–9) Paul surely would have confronted him about it. In Galatians he makes it clear that his difference with the Peter in Jerusalem was a matter of the Mosaic Law, not a matter of a vastly different eschatology. The tone of the 2nd epistle of Peter is far more like the conservative pseudo-Paulines, reflecting a time when the church had become more interested in staying in business than in the impending coming of the Lord. The Peter who was an apostle in Jerusalem probably died somewhere in the 7th decade of the first century.

The first epistle of Peter, which also claims to be written by him, appears to be pre-gospel. Its references to Jesus are sacrificial and expressed in terms of the Passover lamb and the SS. He tells his flock that they are not redeemed by some worthless thing—

> "…but with the precious blood of Christ, as of a lamb without
> blemish and without spot." (1 Pet 1:19)

—Mosaic prerequisites for the Passover lamb. Reminding his sheep of the life of Christ, he paraphrases Isaiah's piece on the SS (1 Pet 2:21–25), adding only the biographical detail that he "bare our sins in his own body on the tree". For those who might think that the author was familiar with the gospel drama of Christ's execution, this precis of Christ's life comes just after he delivered this advice—

> "Submit yourselves to every ordinance of man for the Lord's
> sake, whether it be to the king as supreme, *or unto governors, as*

unto them that are sent by him for the punishment of evildoers,
and for the praise of them that do well." (1 Pet 2:13-4)

The gospels tell us that the governor Pilate ordered the bloody execution of Christ, but this author has no such notion—governors only punish evildoers. His quote from Isaiah includes the words that the SS—Christ—"did no sin", and shortly after he asks—

"And who is he that will harm you, if ye be followers of that which is good?" (3:13)

So is it do no sin and be violently executed, or, do no sin and no one will harm you? This ignorance of the gospel story that the sinless Christ had been juridically executed is consonant with the advice Paul gave to the Romans as illustrated in the last chapter—obey the law and you'll have nothing to fear from the authorities. Sound advice for people living in society in general, but hardly fitting for the followers of a man recently publicly and violently executed as a felon.

There are other letters in the NT that are ascribed to three authors that many believe to have been either disciples or relatives of Jesus. These are John, Jude, and James. But, like the epistles of Paul, these letters also quote none of Jesus' teachings, refer to none of his miracles and say nothing about his life. The first and second letters of John principally warn against deceivers and "anti-Christs" who deny that Jesus is come in the flesh. That Jesus had in very deed "come in the flesh" is asserted numerous times, but the author does not cite any evidence to bolster the case—he rather resorts to threatening the non-believers. We can infer from this that the matter of Jesus' historicity may have been questioned at the time. Had this "John" been a contemporary or near contemporary of Jesus, he could have suggested his readers make an effort to get down to Syria, Galilee, Decapolis, Jerusalem, Judea or Jordan sometime and speak to the innumerable multitudes that witnessed Jesus' sermons and miracles (see e.g. Mt. 4:24–25).

The letter ascribed to James is believed by some to have been written by variously one of the disciples called James, or Jesus' brother, or even his cousin. If the author of this letter knew Jesus, we can only conclude that he failed to make much of an impression on him. He opens by placing the deities "God" and "Jesus Christ" in apposition, refers to himself as a servant of them, and addresses his letter to the "twelve tribes" of Israel. The rest of the letter is full of preaching but makes no reference to Jesus *at all*. When promoting the doctrine of justification by works, he praises the OT cases of Abraham being prepared to murder his son Isaac, and Rahab, who conspired to allow her native city to be invaded. But he bypasses the gospel Jesus who had already given the good word on justification by works—

> "Not everyone that saith unto me, Lord, Lord, shall enter the kingdom of heaven; but he that does the will of my father which is in heaven." (Mt 7:21)

James also reminds his readers of the virtuous patience of the OT hero Job, passing by the authority of Jesus' parable of the seed that fell on good ground—

> "…which is an honest and good heart, having heard the word, keep it, and bring forth fruit with patience." (Lk 8:15b)

He elsewhere writes—

> "But above all things, my brethren, swear not, neither by heaven, neither by the earth, neither by any oath, but let your yay be yay, and your nay, nay; lest ye fall into condemnation." (James 5:12)

Matthew has Jesus counselling something similar to this (Mt 5:37), but James does not cite Jesus as his source. The same teaching is to be found in the Jewish apocryphal *Secrets of Enoch* (44:1–3), where Enoch is giving advice to his sons. The piece quoted from James is more in accord with the wording of Enoch's counsel than it is with that of Matthew's Jesus (see chapter 8 of this book). It is very revealing that when James wants to give an example of a man "subject to like passions as we are" who proved the efficacy of prayer, he cites the case of the OT Elijah who prayed for a flood (James 5:16–18). He could have reminded us that Jesus continually counselled prayer, and is represented in the gospels as frequently withdrawing from company to pray, and as having given specific advice on how to do so (Mt 6:6–13). The reader might note that contemporary preachers constantly stress that *Jesus* was subject to the same temptations that we are, but the notion did not occur to the earliest promoters of the faith.

Another NT epistle regarded as having perhaps been written by one of Jesus' disciples or intimates is that of Jude "the Obscure", labelled thus because no one has any idea who he might have been. He, too, introduces himself as a "servant of Jesus Christ", but then proceeds to draw all his admonitory examples from the OT. He refers to the Israelites' flight from Egypt; a story about angels from Isaiah; the perils of Sodom and Gomorrah; a celestial dispute between Michael the archangel and the devil over the corpse of Moses; Cain; Balaam and his chatty ass (to whom Balaam said "Nay"—see KJV Numbers 22:30); Enoch and even Adam.

He does say that "the *apostles* of our Lord Jesus Christ" said that there would be mockers in the last days (which the author thought he was living in). This prophecy can also be found in 2 Peter 3:3 (this author did *not* believe he was living in the last days. See vs 8–9), but these are not the words of Jesus himself, and Jude does not claim them to be. He implicitly excludes himself from being an apostle, and the fact that he urges his readers recall an apostolic warning suggests a late writing of the epistle. These three authors, then, are the only ones in the NT who have any claim to being of "the twelve" disciples—even if only on the basis as their having the same names as three of them—but they tell us nothing about Jesus himself.

The remaining NT epistle is the anonymous one addressed to "the Hebrews". The author seems particularly enamoured of a mysterious OT figure called Melchizedek—

> "For this Melchizedek, King of Salem, priest of the most high God, who met Abraham returning from the slaughter of the Kings, and blessed him; To whom also Abraham gave a tenth part of all; first being by interpretation King of Righteousness, and after that also King of Salem, which is, King of Peace; Without father, without mother, without descent, having neither beginning of days, nor end of life; but made like unto the Son of God; abideth a priest continually." (Heb. 7:1–3)

We learn that Melchizedek has no parents, no ancestors, no descendants, no beginning and no end, but magically manifests in brief interstices of eternity in some kind of corporeal form, for in Genesis 14:18 he brought forth bread and wine (the Lord's Supper?), and Abraham handed him the tithes. The author of Hebrews likens Jesus to him, saying that Jesus has become a high priest "after the order of Melchizedek". He draws all his teachings and exemplars from the OT, even what he has to say about Jesus, whom he speaks of in mystical and sacrificial terms. He sees great value in the blood of bulls and the ashes of heifers, but asks—

> "How much more shall the blood of Christ, who through the eternal spirit *offered himself* without spot to God, purge your conscience from dead works to serve the living God?" (Heb 9:14. Note in passing: this is a far cry from Jesus being sordidly

murdered by "the Jews" as implied in the text I argued as slan-
derous in the last chapter)

The "without spot", of course, is a Passover lamb requisite. Our author says
that it is evident that "our Lord" sprang out of Juda (meaning he was descended
from the patriarch Judah), but gives no indication that he is doing anything other
than construing this from OT messianic traditions (e.g. Genesis 49:10). When he
speaks in the name of the Lord, it is not Jesus but the OT God he quotes or paraphrases (e.g. Heb 13:5 "he hath said 'I will never leave thee, nor forsake thee'" is
gleaned from such texts as Deuteronomy 31:6, 8 & 1 Chronicles 28:20). He
devotes an entire chapter (ch 11) to a sermon on faith by citing examples of those
who displayed that virtue, but does not mention any of the more contemporary
paragons that *Jesus* praises in the NT. And, almost as if to prove that he knows
none of those gospel traditions, he runs through dozens of the usual OT heroes
and exasperates—

> "What more can I say? For time would fail me to tell of
> Gedeon, and of Barak, and of Samson, and of Jephthae, of
> David also, and Samuel, and of all the prophets" (v 32)

What more indeed. But the author is unique amongst the NT epistle writers
in that he seems to refer to Christ coming *again*, however, like Paul, he is
extremely vague about the time setting of his sacrificial death. He tells us that
because it is appointed unto all men to die—

> "So Christ was once offered to bear the sins of many, and unto
> them that look for him shall he appear the second time with-
> out sin unto salvation." (Heb 9:28)

Once. It probably is not fair to expect an author who believes in supernatural
and supertemporal beings like Melchizedek to feel constrained to be precise
about the timing of an event as cosmic as he considers the sacrifice of Christ to
be. On the venue front we don't fare much better; we are told that Christ "suffered without the gate", but this only seems to be because the Jewish high priest is
duty bound by the Levitical law to burn the carcasses of sacrificed animals "without the camp". Our mystical author even makes it clear that he is speaking figura-
tively, because he then suggests that we proceed to the same destination, "bearing
his reproach" (see Heb 13:11–13).

The Ignorant Fathers

If Paul, James, John, Jude and whoever wrote Hebrews did not know much about the career of the Jesus so beloved of contemporary preachers and American fundamentalist television programs, the Apostolic Father Clement of Rome does not seem to have been much more enlightened. For a long time tradition held that Clement had been Peter's immediate successor in Rome, but he has since been relegated to third place. His epistle to the Corinthians, *1 Clement,* is popularly held to have been written in 95-6 AD in the time of Domitian. There is a possibility that it was written before the destruction of the Jerusalem temple, because the author speaks of the activities of the high priest in Jerusalem as if he were still officiating there. But Josephus also describes the temple ordinances in the present tense after the war (*AJ,* III, 224–236), and it appears that the religious rites were allowed to continue. Clement also refers to members that have been with the Roman church from "youth to old age" (1 Clem 63), so for these and other reasons the general consensus is that it at least belongs to the late 1st century.

Clement should have had a good knowledge of Jesus' life, but he does not appear to have. When he seeks to admonish humility, he nostalgically reminisces on the life of "our Lord Jesus Christ" not by any personally passed on anecdotes by his associates or predecessors, but by quoting the *entire 53rd chapter of Isaiah on the SS*, adding a verse from the Psalms which was also utilised later in constructing the gospel Passion of Christ (1 Clem 16). When he seeks further models for his preaching he resorts exclusively to the OT. He immediately follows the SS admonishment with this—

> "Let us be followers of those who went about in goat-skins and sheep-skins preaching the coming of Christ..."

—and of course the reader, bearing in mind the gospel Jesus, is expecting to hear him praise the great John the Baptist, who as all Christians know—

> "...went about in camel's hair, and with a girdle of skin about his loins... preached, saying, There cometh one mightier than I after me, the latchet of whose shoes I am not worthy to stoop down and unloose." (Mk 1:6–7)

Mark's Baptist is here specifically heralding the coming of Jesus Christ who appears two verses later. But Clement cites the likes of men—

> "…such as Elijah, Eliseus and moreover Ezekiel, the prophets,
> and in addition to them the famous men of old." (1 Clem 17)

Just about everybody *except* the Baptist! The omission of the beloved figure is very telling. Not only is it a reasonable inference that this church leader did not know the gospel story of John heralding the coming of Jesus, it also indicates why the story was made up. When he refers to "the famous men of old", he means the fabulous men from the OT and associated traditions, because, as we shall see, when he mentions Peter and Paul, he refers to them as being from "our own age".

Clement elsewhere admonishes his flock to have faith, and praises that quality in such OT figures as Enoch, Noah, Abraham, Lot and the already-mentioned Rahab—showing how the great faith of all these figures reaped tangible rewards—e.g. Rahab's life was spared; Abraham was granted a son in his sunset years, etc. But he neglects a story much more pertinent to Christians—the sick woman who was healed by faith, merely having to touch Jesus' garment—

> "And he (Jesus) said unto her, Daughter, thy faith hath made
> thee whole; go in peace, and be whole of thy plague." (Mk
> 5:34; Mt 9:22; Lk 8:48)

And why would Clement choose to ignore the story of the Roman centurion who wants Jesus to heal his sick servant, and says to him "say but the word, and my servant shall be healed". Jesus marvels to his disciples at the centurion's attitude—

> "Verily I say unto you, *I have not seen such great faith*, no, not
> in Israel." (Mt 8:10)

He then heals the ailing servant long distance. Here is the Christ—that Clement was supposed to be preaching—specifically declaring this to be the greatest example of faith he ever saw—a faith so strong that it brought immediate reward, vouchsafed by the deity himself. But Clement resorts to the ancient scriptures. His lack of familiarity with the gospel Jesus is even more obvious when he seeks to counsel against jealousy and envy. He writes of the negative consequences of Cain's jealousy for Abel, of how the jealousy of the brothers of the patriarch Joseph brought him into bondage, of how King Saul was brought undone by his envy of David, and of numerous other disastrous OT envy stories. He then says—

> "...but not to insist upon ancient examples, let us come to those worthies that have been nearest to us, and take brave examples of our own age..." (1 Clem 5)

From there he proceeds to give the examples of Peter and Paul, and how through envy they were persecuted and had to endure many sufferings. But he fails to cite the example that should have been foremost in the minds of Clement and his followers if they were at all familiar with the gospels, namely, envy drove the chief priests to persecute and martyr *Jesus*—

> "...for he (Pilate) knew that the chief priests had delivered him (Jesus) for envy." (Mk 15:10; Mt 27:18)

He concludes his sermon on envy with—

> "In a word, envy and strife have overthrown great cities and uprooted mighty nations from the earth." (1 Clem 6)

Here was an excellent opportunity for Clement to mention the gospel allegation that Jerusalem and the temple had been destroyed for the envious murdering of Jesus. What "great city" could have been more important to Clement than Jerusalem, the site of the holy temple and the venue for his Lord's crucifixion? And when it comes to uprooting mighty nations, what example could have been more obvious to Clement than the dispersion of the Jews resulting from that great overthrow? There can be no doubt that he did not know this tradition, which must have been developed later in the 2nd century. This is forceful evidence that the gospels were written after the 1st century, as the earliest gospel Jesus is fully aware that God will destroy Jerusalem as punishment for his own murder (see details next chapter).

Who do the gospels tell us planned and demanded the crucifixion of Jesus? The Sanhedrin under the rule of Caiaphas the High Priest of Jerusalem. He was mortified by Jesus' blasphemy at his trial—

> "Then the High Priest rent his clothes, saying, he has spoken blasphemy, what further need have we of witnesses? Behold, now we have heard his blasphemy. What think ye? They answered and said, he is guilty of death." (Matt 26:65-6)

So the High Priest solicits the death of Jesus. Now, the Christian Clement reminds his flock that the "Master" has set the ordinances for their religious rites—

> "Forasmuch then as these things are manifest beforehand, and we have searched into the depths of the Divine knowledge, we ought to do all things in order, as many as the Master hath commanded us to perform at their appointed seasons…*For unto the High Priest his proper services have been assigned*, and to the priests their proper office is appointed, and upon the Levites their proper ministrations are laid. The layman is bound by the layman's ordinances. Not in every place, brethren, are the continual daily sacrifices offered, or the freewill offerings, or the sin offerings and the trespass offerings, *but in Jerusalem alone.* And even there the offering is not made in every place, but before the sanctuary in the court of the altar; *and this too through the High Priest* and the aforesaid ministers, after that the victim to be offered hath been inspected for blemishes. They therefore who do any thing contrary to the seemly ordinance of His will receive death as the penalty." (vs 40-1)

It might be disturbing to find that Clement is happy that those who disobey the "Master" on punctilious matters of animal sacrifice protocol should be put to death. It is obvious here that the "Master" is the OT God—not Jesus—and by implication Clement is saying that the High Priests in Jerusalem have been doing a jolly good job in the sight of God. Putting aside the problems this raises as to the reformist views of Jesus and his expiation of the need for animal sacrifice, how could Clement praise the performing of the ritual ordinances by the Jerusalem High Priests without lamenting that one of their not too distant predecessors had maliciously engineered the horrific crucifixion of Jesus Christ?

The words of the Lord

Clement does remind his readers to "remember the words of the Lord Jesus", and then cites some teachings that bear similarities to those attributed to Jesus in his

"Sermon on the Mount"—indicating that he may have been aware of the gospel account of Jesus delivering the sermon—

> "Above all, remembering the words of the Lord Jesus, which he spake concerning equity and long suffering, saying, Be ye merciful, and ye shall obtain mercy; forgive, and ye shall be forgiven—as ye do, so shall it be done unto you—as ye judge, so shall ye be judged; as ye are kind to others, so shall God be kind to you—with what measure ye mete, with the same shall it be measured to you again." (1 Clem 13)

It is probable that he was drawing from disembodied teachings of the church. 114 teachings or sayings of Jesus were found near Nag Hamadi in Egypt in 1945. These "sayings of Jesus" are listed discretely, without circumstance or context, introduced with the words "Jesus said…" Many of these sayings resemble things that Jesus is reported to have said in the canonised gospels, where they are applied to definite situations in time and place. Some, however, did not make the grade, like for example where he says that women can only enter the kingdom of heaven if they become males (Thomas 114)! But the existence of these records has led to speculation that the gospel writers may have had access to these and other documents of "sayings of Jesus", *logia*, and that they wrote them into temporal situations when compiling the gospels. Clement tells his flock to—

> "Remember the words of Jesus our Lord. He said—'Woe unto that man! It would have been good for him if he were not born, rather than cause one of my elect to stumble; it would have been better for him to have a millstone hung round him and be sunk in the sea, than to have seduced one of my elect." (Clem 45)

This is the only other time in Clement's letter where he claims to be quoting the words of Jesus. The above threat would appear to be free-floating, as it finds occasion in different contexts in the gospels, and the wording that Clement uses is not the same as the gospel texts. Mark has Jesus use part of it in reference to Judas Iscariot—

> "Woe unto that man through whom the Son of Man is betrayed! Good it were for that man if he had not been born." (Mk 14:21)

And he used another part of it earlier. When holding a young child in his arms, Jesus allegedly said—

> "And whosoever shall offend one of these little ones that believe in me, it is better for him that a millstone were hanged around his neck, and he were cast into the sea." (Mk 9:36–42)

Jesus repeats the same scene again in Mt 18:6 with a child set before him. Luke, curiously, has Jesus say—

> "It is impossible but that offences will come; but woe unto him, through whom they come. It were better for him that a millstone were hanged about his neck, and he cast into the sea, than that he should offend one of these little ones." (Lk 17:1–2)

But the author of Luke, drawing from Mark, has overlooked the detail of having Jesus call any children to him, thus rendering the reference to "these little ones" a little obscure. The use of this "saying", with its distinct tone of damnation, is even more incongruous in Luke as Jesus immediately follows it with the admonition to his disciples to forgive their trespassing brothers "seven times a day" if necessary. In the first example given here, Jesus' use of the saying is bizarre, as he said it right in front of Judas who we have to believe, as noted earlier, didn't bat an eye-lid at the terrible threat. Clement's wording is a rough combination of the two above cited texts from Mark. (This can also mean that Mark split the "saying" in two.) If Clement knew that the "better if he had not been born" piece had been applied specifically to Judas Iscariot by the Lord himself, it would seem strange that he should attach it to the other similar sounding threat which designates *anyone* who might cause the elect to "stumble", as it would undermine the gravity of Jesus' damning words. In the second and third cases (Mk 9:42 & Lk 17:1–2) we are asked to believe that Jesus was trying to convert little children to his obscure cause that—according to the gospels themselves—even his disciples did not understand. And the usage of the saying by Luke's Jesus is essentially contradictory to the pious teaching that immediately follows it. Was Jesus so confused? Or does all this make more sense if the gospel writers made use of certain pre-existing pneumatic "sayings of Jesus"—compiled over time by the priests of the sect—and consequently created situations in their biographies of Jesus to accommodate them, however awkwardly?

This "woe unto that man" threat against those who might cause the elect to stumble may even have been created by Clement, or his colleagues, to intimidate heretics and rebels within the sect in his own day. Further on in the epistle he tellingly writes—

> "Should any disobey *what has been said by Him* (Jesus) *through us*, let them understand that they will entangle themselves in no small transgression and danger." (*Lightfoot*, 1 Clem 59)

So the leaders of the early church were mouthpieces through which "Jesus" delivered his teachings and commandments. His words appear to have come to us via pneumatic utterances, direct revelation, in similar fashion to how Clement's spiritual mentor Paul boasted he was contacted (and presumably likewise for the other apostles Paul mentions). Clement does not claim to have gleaned knowledge about Jesus' teachings from written gospels, but from the preaching of an unspecified number of apostles, who received their teachings from Jesus Christ. He tells us that they were "assured by the resurrection of our Lord Jesus Christ" (1 Clem 42), but this does not imply personal knowledge of an earthly Jesus by anybody, because he includes Paul as an apostle (v 47), and we know that Paul was only assured of the resurrection of Jesus Christ by a heavenly vision. Peter (Cephas) is also described as an apostle, but again, not because he knew Jesus, but for his "high reputation" (same verse)—the definition of an apostle we saw in the chapter on Paul. So Clement's epistle is not inconsistent with the theory that no teachings were ever delivered by an earthly Jesus, and that the only biography the earliest Church writers knew of Jesus was what they construed from the SS text of Isaiah. It is true that they generally regarded Christ as having been crucified, but this particular fate for the SS—whose means of death is unspecified and who had to die somehow—was probably evoked by meditating on the dummy attached to the tree borne in the Attis festival. It is interesting to note that, whilst Clement was aware of at least some of Paul's writings, he never uses the verb or adjective "crucified"—which Paul does repeatedly.

Somewhere about this time appears the enigmatic epistle of Barnabas, one that is very difficult to date with any great precision. It contains some traditions that concur and some that conflict with our gospels (e.g. he regards the doctrine that Christ should descend from David as the teaching of "evil" men). He tells us that an earthly Jesus chose his own apostles, but sadly does not furnish their names. He says in one place that Jesus worked miracles, but unfortunately gives us no descriptions of them; and he says that Jesus taught, but alas gives us no details just what. He asserts that Christ came in the flesh—

> "Moreover, teaching Israel, and doing so great miracles and signs, He preached to them and loved them greatly. But when He chose His own apostles who were to preach His Gospel, he chose those that were iniquitous above all sin, that He might show He came 'not to call the righteous, but sinners to repentance.' Then He manifested Himself to be the Son of God. For if He had not come in the flesh, how could men have been saved by beholding Him? (Barn 5:8–10)

It is not clear here if the quote is supposed to be from Jesus or from some scripture. Note that it was for theological reasons that Christ had to come in the flesh. Although Barnabas' epistle is lengthy he provides *no names of anybody involved in Christ's life* and mentions no venues for anything he might have done; he construes all of his ideas about him from the OT. He too relies heavily upon Isaiah's SS—

> "For to this end the Lord endured to deliver up His flesh to corruption, that we might be sanctified through the remission of sins, which is effected by His blood of sprinkling. For it is written concerning Him, partly with reference to Israel, and partly to us; and the Scripture saith thus: '*He was wounded for our transgressions, and bruised for our iniquities: with His stripes we are healed. He was brought as a sheep to the slaughter, and as a lamb which is dumb before its shearer.*' Therefore we ought to be deeply grateful to the Lord, *because He has both made known to us things that are past*, and hath given us wisdom concerning things present, and hath not left us without understanding in regard to things which are to come." (Barn 5:1–3)

Barnabas explicitly says that the Lord has revealed the details of Christ's sacrifice through Isaiah, which was written at least two centuries before his time. So much for eyewitnesses. We would hardly need to thank the Lord for apprising us of that information if we knew those details independently. Barnabas is the OT exegete *par excellence.* He clearly believes that Christ was affixed to a cross, and sees references to it everywhere in the OT, even in the numerological significance of Abraham's circumcision activities (Barn 9:7). But contrary to the gospels, he ascribes the inauguration of all the familiar rituals of Christianity, such as baptism, to Moses and associated OT heroes.

Jesus dons human clothing

The earliest traceable details of Jesus' biography do come to us from the church father Ignatius, who in bondage wrote his seven evangelical epistles to seven churches sometime after Clement, probably in 115 AD when he was (very willingly) executed, incidentally, not for being a Christian *per se*, but for suspicion of causing Antioch's catastrophic earthquake of that year. (His Roman jailers would hardly have allowed him to write and post his letters stridently promoting the cause he had been arrested for!) Ignatius tells us that Jesus came into the world via parthenogenesis and that his mother's name was Mary. He claimed Jesus to be of the line of King David, and that he was persecuted and crucified in the time of Pontius Pilate. Unlike earlier writers, he is at pains to stress some base realities of Jesus' mundane existence, but doesn't provide any detail of his life between his birth and his crucifixion.

Ignatius and his colleagues may have contrived these minimalist details to confute the Docetists, who reasoned that if Jesus were fully divine he could only have suffered voluntarily. They could not believe that an omnipotent deity would subject himself to such a thing, so they decided that Jesus must only have *appeared* to suffer. The more materialistic Christians sensed danger in this concept and wanted to fill the lacunae, so Ignatius assures his readers that Christ was "truly born", "truly persecuted", "truly nailed up in the flesh" and "truly rose from the dead" (see e.g. Trallians 9 & Smyrneans 1). As I have sought to demonstrate, the earlier Christian writers, when sermonising on suffering and persecution, pass Jesus by and either employ OT examples or the experiences of Peter and Paul.

Ignatius appears to have been familiar with aspects of Matthew's gospel, but he does not specifically quote from Matthew, and he doesn't purely rely on Matthew for events that Matthew covered. For example, his description of the "star in the East" which heralded the birth of Jesus—

> "…and all the other stars, with the sun and the moon, became
> a chorus for that star, which outshone them all…" (Eph 19)

—reads more like the dream that the patriarch Joseph had about himself—

> "Behold, I have dreamed a dream more; and behold, the sun
> and the moon and the eleven stars made obeisance to me."
> (Gen 37:9)

—than it does of the account given in Matthew, where only a single star in the east is mentioned. This is a fairly typical example of how the early Christian writers delved into the Hebrew traditions to find scriptural precedents for miraculous signs to attribute to the life of Jesus. Some wording used in Ignatius' writings parallels wording ascribed to Jesus in the gospels, but he doesn't quote Jesus when he uses this material, and it is usually blended in with other ideas. For example, he writes—

> "For if the prayers of one or two be of such force, as we are
> told; how much more powerful shall that of the bishop and the
> whole church be?" (Ephesians 2)

"As we are told" does not sound like the kind of phrasing that he would use if he thought the speaker was Jesus. Matthew has Jesus say—

> "Again I say unto you, that if two of you shall agree on earth as
> touching anything that they shall ask, it shall be done for them
> of my father which is in heaven." (Mt 18:19)

The teaching that Matthew attributes to Jesus deals with the idea of an agreement between two men being binding before God, whereas Ignatius was trying to induce his readers to go to church (something the gospel writers could hardly make Jesus do). In any event he does not claim Jesus as his authority, so some parallels in his wording with that of the gospel Jesus could be because the respective writers were using the priestly idiom of the times. The words were probably attributed to Jesus retrospectively.

The church father Polycarp knew of Ignatius' epistles, and wrote his own epistle to the Philippians probably somewhere between 115 and 135 AD. He appears to quote a similar section of the "beatitudes" that are used in Matthew, and the saying Jesus uses in the Garden of Gethsemane, "the spirit is willing, but the flesh is weak". It is generally agreed that he had access to some form of Matthew, and perhaps some form of Luke. This is certainly possible, as these gospels were definitely extant in the latter half of the 2nd century. The versions he had, however, could not have been the same as those we have today. In the middle of the 2nd century Justin Martyr still thought that Jesus was born in a cave (*Dialogue* 78), and so did Origen in the early 3rd century (Bk 1:51).

Briefly then, Clement in the late 1st century, like the letters of Paul, Peter, James, Jude, John and "Hebrews", tells us nothing of Jesus' biography that does not accord with Isaiah's SS. He does not specify whether he believed that the few words of Jesus he quotes were spoken by Jesus on earth or inspirationally through the church leaders. He concentrates more on the idea of resurrection, points to the cycles of the seasons to promote this and even resorts to the example of "the Lord" raising the Phoenix from its cinders every five hundred years as evidence for the phenomenon. All these writers uphold specific ideas and teachings with are incongruous with our received gospels. It is not until the early decades of the 2nd century, with Ignatius and then Polycarp after him, that a more cohesive tradition of Jesus' biography—replete with dates, venues and names—begins to emerge.

Secular References

There are no historians contemporary with Jesus that report on him, so we now have to look in later writers. The only references to him as such are two in the writings of Josephus. This man was born of a priestly family in Jerusalem in 37 AD and during the Roman/Jewish war switched sides to the Romans. After the war he lived in Rome and wrote an early account of the war by about 75 AD. He also wrote an autobiography and a polemic against the Greek Apion, but his major work was the *Antiquities of the Jews* (completed around 93 AD), which traced the history of the Jews from the beginning of the world till the end of the Roman/Jewish war.

The first reference to Jesus in *Antiquities* is where the historian details uprisings amongst the Jews during the prefecture of Pontius Pilate—

> "About this time there lived Jesus, a wise man, if indeed one ought to call him a man. For he was one who wrought surprising feats and was a teacher of such people as accept the truth gladly. He won over many Jews and many of the Greeks. He was the Messiah. When Pilate, upon hearing him accused by men of the highest standing amongst us, had condemned him to be crucified, those who had in the first place come to love him did not give up their affection for him. On the third day he appeared to them restored to life, for the prophets of God had prophesied these and countless other marvellous things

about him. And the tribe of Christians, so called after him, has still to this day not disappeared." (*Ant* XVIII, 63-4)

This text is contested on many grounds. First of all, earlier in the same chapter Josephus cited only the Sadducees, Pharisees, Essenes and Zealots as the sects amongst the Jews right up till the nationalist revolt against the Romans. He terminates his descriptions of them with "these, then, are the sects amongst the Jews" (see XVIII, 11–25). Also, Josephus was not a Christian, so he would not have written that Jesus was the Messiah. We know for a fact that the text has been doctored, because Origen, who read Josephus, specifically states that Josephus did not believe Jesus was the Christ (*Contra Celsum* I, 47). This does not necessarily imply that Josephus wrote something *else* about Jesus; Origen is rather affirming that he was not a Christian.

Our received text purports that Josephus claimed that "men of the highest standing amongst us" accused Jesus, without specifying what the allegations were, suspiciously similar to the way the gospel Passion accounts do. He does not even proffer a reason for why they should have condemned Jesus. The reference to Jesus reappearing on the third day and the prophets predicting events of his life reads like a doctrinal statement.

But the major problem with the text is that it breaks the continuity of Josephus' writing. At first he writes of how, as noted in chapter one of this book, Pilate had brought statues of Tiberius from Caesarea to Jerusalem and placed some in the temple. This caused a revolt amongst the Jews, and only when Pilate saw how they were prepared to die rather than have their temple defiled did he relent and send the statues back to Caesarea. Then he tells of how Pilate raided the temple funds to build an aqueduct into Jerusalem. When the populace protested, he dressed Roman soldiers in civvies with concealed daggers. The crowd refused to disperse, so at a given signal the soldiers set upon them, and "many of them were actually slain on the spot, while some withdrew disabled by blows. Thus ended the uprising". Skip the above paragraph on Jesus, and the next verse begins with—

"About this time another outrage threw the Jews into an uproar…"

—providing continuity, as the paragraph on Jesus mentions no uproar. He goes on to tell of a scandal in the temple of Isis in Rome, and follows it with a report on how four thousand Jews were evicted from Rome on account of the behaviour of four. As noted earlier, there is not a skerrick of evidence of any outrage or revolt arising from the death of Jesus, and this received Josephan description of his death provides none. The whole piece is widely regarded as a late Christian interpolation, including by many theologians. The outrage is implied because that is the opinion of the interfering Christian.

The other contested Josephan reference to Jesus occurs, almost in passing, where the historian tells of how Agrippa II, in 62 AD, had appointed a certain Ananus to the High Priesthood. Josephus details him as rash in temper, and of the school of the Sadducees whom he describes as—

> "...very rigid in judging offenders, above all the rest of the Jews...he (Ananus) convened the judges of the Sanhedrin, and brought before them a man called James, the brother of Jesus, him called Christ, and certain others. He accused them of having transgressed the law and delivered them up to be stoned."
> (*Ant* XX, 200)

Josephus reports that some good citizens were outraged at Ananus' actions and complained to King Agrippa. A delegation even went to protest to the procurator Albinus that it had been unlawful for Ananus to convene the Sanhedrin without his consent. Albinus concurred with them and wrote an angry letter to Ananus threatening him with punishment, and Agrippa deposed him and replaced him with Jesus the son of Damneus (see vs 197–203).

Was Christ now so well known and respected by the authorities in Jerusalem at this time that they would immediately punish someone who harmed one of his relatives? Exactly what had transpired to make Christianity, and Jesus' relatives, so acceptable? Or is "the brother of Jesus who was called Christ" an interpolation? There are good reasons to suspect so. Importantly, Bishop Clement could have pointed to the malicious treatment of such a prestigious Christian figure in his late 1st century listing of tragic strife and envy stories. If the story were true it is unlikely that Clement would not have known about it. That he did not mention the persecution of *the very brother of Jesus Christ* is almost as serious as his failure to mention the persecution of Jesus himself. This atrocity, as noted, occurred in 62 AD. Paul arrived in Rome either in 59 or 60 AD, and Acts tells us that he stayed in his own hired house for two years. Acts had to be written some time after this, so it is also curious that its author did not mention the unlawful killing of this James "the brother of Jesus".

The Josephan text has definitely undergone some doctrinal treatment. Writing about 200 AD, Origen opined (*Contra Celsum* I, 47) that Josephus was incorrect in attributing the cause of the fall of Jerusalem and the destruction of the temple to a punishment for the killing of James the Just, and that he should rather have attributed it to a punishment for the killing of Jesus proper. Origen himself does not make it clear whether he means that Josephus thought the Romans punished "the Jews" for this, or whether God did, or a combination of both. However, the fact that he would have liked to have seen the cause referred to the killing of Jesus indicates he has divine punishment in mind, for he could hardly be suggesting that the *Romans* would be so incensed at the execution of Jesus that they would destroy the country.

But the problem is that Josephus says nothing like this in the manuscripts we have today. So either Origen misconstrued the Josephan text—which is extremely unlikely as he would have pored over anything in Josephus that sounded like an allusion to Jesus—or there was a different version of the story circulating in Origen's time wherein "Josephus" did proffer some such opinion. However, an opinion of that order is obviously a point of Christian propaganda. Origen says "the Jews...put him (James) to death", but "the Jews" no more put James to death than "the Americans" killed John Kennedy, or "the Hindus" killed Gandhi. The murder of James was orchestrated by some Sanhedrin rogues, and it was a delegation of Jewish citizens that protested it to the governor. Furthermore, the Jewish king Agrippa punished them for it. If it is true that another version of Josephus boasted such an opinion it must have been an earlier Christian insertion. Origen even fantasizes that Josephus furnished us with this point of view *contre-coeur*. The notion that Josephus would feel compelled to opine that the whole nation should be destroyed for a crime—by some Jews against a Christian Jew—which had already been punished by other Jews, borders on the absurd. Josephus was not "anti-semitic"; he makes clear his view that it was the Zealot rebellion against Roman rule—provoked by bad governors—which led to the disaster. Ultimately, the fact that there were different versions of the story circulating from an early time renders our received text unreliable.

It is well known there was a James who was very prominent in the early Jerusalem cult, and the 2nd century church believed him to be the sibling of Jesus. As the James mentioned in Josephus is described as righteous and his execution depicted as unjust, the 2nd century Church may have claimed this James as one of their own, identifying him with the James of the Jerusalem Church referred to in Paul's letter to the Galatians. This would explain why Clement apparently did not know anything about it, and its similar exclusion from *Acts* (oddly enough, *Acts* reports the killing of a *different* James). Once the tradition was established that the unjustly executed James in Josephus' history was Jesus' brother, a Christian copyist could have added the gloss identifying him as the brother of Jesus.

This reference to James, with all its detail, further highlights the incongruous piety and brevity of Josephus' earlier piece on Jesus. Notice that no one was sacked for the greater atrocity, even though in the gospels Pilate is portrayed as showing sympathy for Jesus. My suspicion is that the treatment of this James inspired some details of the gospel depiction of the condemnation of Jesus, even replete with the notion of an unlawfully convened Sanhedrin (mirroring the booby-trapped Ides Senate meeting) and a sympathetic governor. The Roman appointed governor and the Jewish king were swift to act on the side of decency in the case of this James. How much more diligently should they have acted in the case of Jesus? The gospel writers could not fake history to the extent of having the High Priest Caiaphas sacked, so the best they could come up with was to have the untraceable Joseph of Arimathea approach governor Pilate for permission to take Jesus' body, so that he and the likewise untraceable Nicodemus could provide him with a decent burial.

Later References

Suetonius, writing around 116-7 AD of the reign of Claudius (41–54 AD), tells us that—

> "Because the Jews at Rome caused continual disturbances at
> the instigation of Chrestus, he expelled them from the city."
> (*Life of Claudius* XXV)

Some have taken this *Chrestus* to be Jesus, but this cannot be clearly established. Chrestus was a common name in Rome at the time, but it is possible that Suetonius meant to write *Christus,* meaning Messiah. *Acts* tells us "Claudius had commanded all the Jews to depart from Rome" (Acts 18:2) but does not give us the reason. Why should Jewish Christians have been causing disturbances? This "Chrestus" may have been the name of a revolutionary cell, or, just as it sounds, a militant agitator then living in Rome who was stirring the Jews to rebellious activities which led to their partial expulsion by Claudius. In any case it is not a clear reference to the gospel Jesus. In another chapter, when listing various reforms enacted by Nero (54–68 AD), he wrote—

> "Punishments were also inflicted on the Christians, a sect pro-
> fessing a new and mischievous superstition." (Suet *Nero*, 16)

It is unfortunate that he did not tell us more about the superstition. Neither of these Suetonian references sound like the kind of pious communities that Paul thought he was writing to in Rome, whose "faith is spoken of throughout the whole world" (Romans 1:8). This matter troubled Gibbon, and he conjectured, and stressed that it was conjecture, that the Jews referred to were more likely to be supporters of the Zealot school of Judas of Galilee (or "the Gaulonite"), confused with Christians by Suetonius. The early Christian writings are demonstrably quietistic. But it is probable that in Rome, just as in Palestine, militant Jews were revolting against Roman rule. In any event, the reference tells us nothing about Jesus himself.

A more elaborate version of the Neronian punishments appears in Tacitus. Writing shortly after Suetonius on the burning of Rome in 64 AD, Tacitus claims that rumours were flying thick and fast that Nero himself had set fire to Rome, so to divert suspicion—

> "...he shifted the charge onto others, and inflicted the most cruel tortures onto a body of men detested for their abominations, and popularly known by the name of Christians. This name came from one Christus, who was put to death in the reign of Tiberius by the procurator Pontius Pilate; but though checked for the time, the detestable superstition broke out again, not in Judea only, where the mischief began, but even in Rome, where every horrible and shameful iniquity, from every quarter of the world, pours in and finds a welcome." (*Annals* XV, 44)

He goes on to say that a vast number of these people were condemned "not so much on the charge of incendiarism as for their hatred of the human race". They were torn to pieces by dogs, attached to crosses, or burned to provide light when daylight failed. Tacitus obviously did not like Nero; it is difficult to believe that blazing Christian bodies would be used as night-lights. At the time of Tacitus' writing, some Christians had assumed the view that the world was the evil domain of Satan that was soon coming to a catastrophic end. (Such a view is promoted in the contentious NT book *Revelations,* which reads like a reworked Jewish apocalypse) This failed to endear them to non-Christians, who did not keen to the notion that they were the minions of Satan.

But the punishments still sound too severe. Tacitus may have gleaned his information on Christians being punished under Nero from Suetonius, and he could have retrojected persecution stories he had heard of Christians in his own time, filling in the gaudy details by giving free rein to his imagination to blacken the name of Nero. This reference by Tacitus to *Christus* being put to death by the procurator Pilate is late and unreliable. Had he been drawing from a state record of Jesus' execution, he should have referred to Pilate correctly as a prefect, not a procurator, and would have furnished us with the real name of Jesus rather than the title *Christus*—messiah—as if it were a man's name. As Wells has observed, he would hardly have found an official document reading "We killed the Messiah this morning", so he must have had another source of information. We know from Ignatius that before the time of Tacitus' writing Christians already held the view that Pilate had presided over the death of Jesus. The fact that the historian Tacitus uses the word *Christus* indicates that he obtained his information from what the Christians themselves believed, and reported it in the same way that a Westerner might relate that Buddhists follow the teachings of prince Gautama, who lived in a palace till he abandoned his sheltered life, experienced four consciousness-shattering visions and sat down under a Bo tree awaiting enlightenment. The issue of whether the story of Gautama is actually true is not usually considered when Westerners make passing references to what Buddhists believe.

The earliest indubitable mention of Christians by a disinterested party comes from Pliny the Younger, who was propraetor of Pontus and Bithynia circa 112 AD when some Christians came before him for trial. He sought advice from the emperor Trajan on how to proceed. He complained about their "degenerate practices" and suspected that they might be a political society, and the matter of their fealty to the Roman state was his primary concern, and consequently his report throws no light on Jesus proper (see *Pliny to Trajan*, Letter XCVI).

Briefly then, none of these non-Christian writers provide us with any information on the life of Jesus, but are rather references to messianic Jews or Christians, and a late statement of the latter's belief, which was then extant, by Tacitus—that "Christus" (not Jesus of Nazareth; bar Joseph etc) had been put to death under Pilate.

But another disturbing problem in the search for the historical Jesus is presented by the writers who should have mentioned him, but did not. Apart from Josephus, the Jewish theoretician and historian Philo of Alexandria also wrote on Jewish affairs, both political and religious. The date of his birth is uncertain, but he died somewhere between 45–50 AD. He made at least one journey through Palestine and was present in Jerusalem for at least one Passover. He provides information on the Essenes, for example, but makes no reference to Jesus. In this connection it should also be said that Jesus is not mentioned in the Dead Sea scrolls, although there have been some strenuous and inventive attempts to find him there.

A more damning omission would seem to be that of the not so well known Justus of Tiberias, a denizen of the arena in question. This Jewish historian penned an account of the Roman/Jewish war, and a history of all the kings of the Jews right up till the time of Agrippa II. His works are no longer extant, but he wrote a detailed account of the events leading up to the destruction of Jerusalem, as can be construed by responses in Josephus' autobiography to allegations Justus made about his activities in the war, i.e. that of stirring up Jewish nationalism. He covered the period in which Jesus allegedly lived, as can be inferred in a comment by the 9th century Christian father Photius of Constantinople, who read his work—

> "Dearest Tarasius…(I)…read the *Chronicle* of Justus of Tiberias…he uses very concise language, and he omits a great deal which is of the utmost importance. Being of the Jewish prejudice, as indeed he was himself also born a Jew, he makes not the least mention of the appearance of Christ, or the things that happened to him, or of the wonderful works he did."
> (*Bibliotheca*, code 33)

Unlike the Jewish Josephus, who Origen thought felt constrained to grudgingly present a Christian-friendly explanation for the destruction of Jerusalem, Photius thinks that Justus deliberately ignored Jesus' existence. But would a Jewish researcher of the future, writing a political history of the 20th century, not mention Hitler, for example, because he did not approve of him? It may have been Jewish prejudice, but on the other hand it may be that Justus never heard of Jesus at all. He should have, though, because (a) the gospels tell us Jesus was executed for regal pretensions, so it would have been pertinent to his subject matter, and (b) Tiberias, where he hailed from, was a town on the Sea of Galilee, and according to John's gospel large crowds came from *this very city* by boat to hear Jesus preach (see Jn 6:1, 2, 22, 23). And it was located only a few miles from Capernaum, where Mark reports that Jesus strode into the synagogue to hold court—

> "…and they were astonished at his doctrine…" (Mk 1:21-2)

Jesus then proceeded to cure a man of an unclean spirit, and—

> "…they were all amazed, insomuch that they questioned among themselves, saying, What thing is this? And immedi-

ately his fame spread abroad throughout *all the region* round about Galilee..." (Mk 1:27-8)

He performs another miracle, and at sunset—

"...*all the city* was gathered together at the door." (Mk 1:33)

Then follows a whistle-stop tour through all the synagogues of Galilee. Jesus "casts out devils" and miraculously cures a leper who—

"...went out, and began to publish it much, and to blaze abroad the matter, *insomuch that Jesus could no more enter the city.*" (1:45)

But he *does* return to Capernaum, and as soon as the word gets out that he's in "the house"—

"...straightway many were gathered together, inasmuch as *there was no room to receive them*, no, not so much as about the door." (2:1–2)

Matthew tells us—

"...and Jesus went about Galilee, teaching in their synagogues...*and his fame went all through Syria*...and there followed him great multitudes of people from Galilee, and from Decapolis, and from Jerusalem, and from Judea, and from beyond Jordan." (Mt 4:24-5)

Finally, Luke tells us that at one of Jesus' meetings—

"...there were gathered together an *innumerable multitude* of people, *insomuch that they trod on one another.*" (Lk 12:1)

What the gospel authors are alleging is that Jesus was an instant superstar. It is probably safe to assume some exaggeration on their part.

When in Rome...

The very nature and form of Christianity, arising as it did shortly after all the dust generated by the Roman civil wars had settled, is part and parcel of the cultural milieu of the Pax Romana. This includes the notion of a gospel. The Greek word translated *gospel* (formerly godspel) is *euangelion*, meaning "good message" or "good news". A decree issued in the year 9 BC by the Provincial Assembly of Asia Minor in honour of Caesar Augustus reads in part—

> "Whereas the Providence which has guided our whole existence and which has shown such care and liberality, has brought our life to the peak of perfection in giving to us Augustus Caesar, whom it filled with virtue for the welfare of mankind, and who, being sent to us and to our descendants as a *saviour,* has put an end to war and has set all things in order; and whereas, having become manifest, Caesar has fulfilled all the hopes of earlier times, and finally that the birthday of the God (Augustus) has been for the whole world the beginning of the *gospel* (euangelion) concerning him, (therefore, let all reckon a new era beginning from the date of his birth.)" (*Ancient Roman Religion.* F C Grant. Lib Arts Press, 1957. p 174)

Here we see the notion clearly expressed that Augustus, the appointed heir and "son" of Caesar, was regarded as a saviour who came down from heaven to perform a specific task, and the proclamation of that mission was called a gospel. Julius Caesar was regarded as having descended from the gods, performed a mission, and returned there. Commenting on Caesar's dignity in covering himself on the point of death "when his divine spirit was being separated from his mortal body", the Roman moralist Valerius Maximus wrote—

> "Mortal men do not expire in such a manner, but that is the way the eternal gods return to their abodes." (IV.5.6.)

The Romans regarded the realm of the gods as both physical and spiritual. Manilius—

> "Augustus has come down from heaven and one day will occupy it, guiding its passage through the zodiac with the Thunderer (Jupiter) at his side; in the assembly of the gods he will behold mighty Quirinus (Romulus) *and him whom he himself has dutifully added as a new deity to the powers above, on a higher plane than shines the belt of the Milky Way.*" (Bk I, 799–802)

The italicised piece refers to Caesar, as confirmed by—

> "Unconquered be the Father of the Fatherland, may Rome serve none but him, for in that she has given a god to heaven, may she miss him not on earth!" (Bk I, 925-6)

Rome has given the god Caesar to heaven, and she will not miss him on earth because the divine Augustus reigns in his stead. Is it surprising that this is the historical period in which the Christ is set? Manilius has it that it was preordained that Caesar should die and he even provides a possible starting point for a link to the doctrine of salvation through the blood of Christ—

> "When after his victory and happy settlement of civil strife he was administering the laws of peace, even he who was born of heaven and was to heaven restored could not escape the violence so oft foretold—before the eyes of the assembled Senate he obliterated with his own blood the evidence of the plot and the list of the conspirators which he held in his hand—all this so that fate could prevail." (Bk IV, 57–62)

And of course the plaque at Ephesus—mentioned earlier—pronouncing Caesar as "God made manifest", testifies to the perception of him as a pre-existing divinity. So the gospel of *divus iulius* would have run along these lines: the Saviour of mankind descended from heaven and manifested in human form, put an end to war and strife, instituted a policy of reform and *clementia*, was betrayed and abandoned by his countrymen and blotted out the names of the guilty with his blood, and then returned to the heavens from whence he came. This is the infrastructure around which I maintain the Christ myth was formed. Gibbon, no fan of the Caesars, had this to say—

> "Even the character of Caesar or Augustus were (sic) far superior to those of the popular deities. But it was the misfortune of the former to live in an enlightened age, and their actions were too faithfully recorded to admit of such a mixture of fable and mystery as the devotion of the vulgar requires. As soon as their divinity was established by law, it sunk into oblivion, without contributing either to their own fame, or to the dignity of succeeding princes." (Gibbon, ch 3)

I see no reason to disagree with Gibbon here, except that Caesar's divinity was originally a popular perception and was only ratified by law later. My suggestion is that the authors of our gospels provided the vulgar with the "fable and mystery" that could not be attached to the vita of the true founder of the Empire precisely because he was real. They had the privilege of the free hand that the faithful recorders of history do not.

Days of Wine and Water

So there are many things written in the biographies of the gospel Jesus that are plainly fantastic, and they are there to fulfil certain expectations of what the *vita* of a deity should be, and also to promote doctrines that were created by the evolving church. They contain mostly Roman, Hebrew and Greek elements. The first century of our era was the age of miracles. It is plain that exorcism was widely believed in by Jews (a la Mark's gospel), and many believed in physical resurrection and that Elijah and the Hebrew saints were about to appear on earth amidst much blasting of trumpets. This credulity was by no means restricted to the Jews, as there were mystics and sooth-sayers wandering the length and breadth of the Roman Empire. Philostratus later wrote a lengthy account of the fabulous life and times of the 1st century sage and miracle worker Apollonius of Tyana, and even the staid emperor Tiberius was believed to have had the gift of *instantly* healing crippled bodies—just like Christ. Tacitus tells us of the mania for prophecy in the late Roman Republic and the early Empire, and Suetonius also remarked on the worldwide obsession for it.

Such an environment is obviously prime breeding ground for tall tales. Unfortunately our gospels are not internally coherent documents, which makes it difficult to break down the material in a coherent fashion. So in this chapter I rather want to point out some of the clearer evidences of creative and fictive writings in them, and highlight a strange dichotomy they display.

Paul preached a crucified Christ, but his real concern was to promote the idea that Christ rose from the dead as the centrepiece of his soteriology. So Paul's "Christ" has the most minimal of earthly biographies. He holds him to have been "made of a woman" (no virgin birth as yet) with no further details provided. This is consistent with the SS, because the Isaiahan text says "For he shall grow up before him as a tender plant and as a root out of dry ground."—therefore he would need to have had a mother. All that Paul was really trying to establish was that Jesus had a physical form before being glorified, otherwise, in his thinking, the faithful would have no hope of resurrection. The package-deal promotion was that Jesus "died (the earthly body) and rose again (the glorified body)".

It is obvious that Ignatius had no official record of a Christian community dating from prior to the time of Pilate, and Pilate was hated by his subjects for his slaughtering of Jews during nationalist and religious disturbances. So the period of his prefecture provided a window for Mark to set the Passion of Christ in historical time. As the earliest gospel, in keeping with the mythological theory, it is quite brief. There is still no virgin birth, no dramatic perinatal speeches or visits by wise men from the East; no herald angels or fanfare—just bang!—Jesus appears on the earth as a full-grown man on the banks of the Jordan and is baptised by John. He then proceeds to "astonish" the crowds in Galilee with his teachings and miracles. The positive aspects of the teachings of the gospel Jesus are generally Pharisaic, and can be dealt with in a few brief paragraphs. If Jesus truly had something astonishing to say we might have hoped Mark would tell us about it. But any of the teachings in Mark that have any ethical value can be found in pre-existing traditions.

He gives us no Sermon on the Mount, for example, and most of the early part of his gospel is spent establishing Jesus' divinity by way of serial miracles and exorcisms (for the vulgar). On the ethical side, in chapter seven he makes Jesus condemn adulteries, fornications, murders, thefts, covetings, wickedness, deceit, lasciviousness, an evil eye, blasphemy, pride and foolishness. Such prohibitions are part of the general wisdom of mankind. Denouncing human vice is hardly profound and certainly not new. Imagine being astonished, for example, at someone telling you not to be "wicked". Such preaching would buy no arguments with either the Pharisees or the Sadducees of his time.

Setting aside the lack of anything astounding in the ethical teachings of Jesus, any virtue in his advice "sell what thou hast, and give to the poor" is negated by the promise that those who do "will have treasure in heaven"—which makes giving to the poor sound like a profitable business (Mk 10:21). For those who might object that Jesus was referring to *spiritual* treasure, not so. Further on he says—

> "…there is no man who has left house, or brethren or sisters, or mother or father or children for my sake and for the gospel's sake, *but that he shall receive a hundredfold in this time,* houses and brethren, and sisters, and mothers, and children, and lands, with persecutions (?), and in the world to come eternal life." (Mk 10:29–30)

Why should anyone have to forsake house, brethren and land if Jesus was preaching simple virtues, pious living, and a code that the world should live by? Josephus tells us that in 6 AD, when Judea was annexed to Syria, the new governor, Cyrenius, proceeded with a property assessment to facilitate taxation. As mentioned earlier, a man named Judas led a revolt against the authorities. He seized a cache of Roman weapons and fled to the wilds of Galilee. Hence he became known as Judas of Galilee, or more simply, "the Galilean". Here he mustered support and founded the Zealots, who from that time on waged a guerilla war against the Romans and what they saw as their Jewish puppets. This is the sect that Gibbon thought Suetonius might have confused with the Christians. Josephus gave us a description of them—

> "As for the fourth of the philosophies (of the Jews), Judas the Galilaean set himself up as leader of it. This school agrees in all other respects with the opinions of the Pharisees, except that they have a passion for liberty that is almost unconquerable, since they are convinced that God alone is their master. They think little of submitting to death in unusual forms and permitting vengeance to fall on kinsmen and friends if only they may avoid calling any man master. In as much as most people have seen the steadfastness of their resolution amid such circumstances, I may forgo any further account. For I have no fear that anything reported of them will be considered incredible. The danger is rather, that report may minimise the indifference with which they accept the grinding misery of pain. The folly that ensued began after Gessius Florus, who was governor, had by his overbearing and lawless actions provoked a desperate rebellion against the Romans." (*AJ,* XVIII, 23-5)

The folly that he refers to is the Roman/Jewish war (note in passing he says nothing about the killing of "James the Just"). Judas had attracted a large rebel following, and his bands not only attacked Roman soldiers but fell on their quisling countrymen as well. He established a kind of rogue dynasty, and his descendants and followers carried on the fight for liberation. Two of his sons, Simon and Jacob, were crucified under Tiberius Alexander somewhere between 45–48 AD. The Greeks of Caesarea Maritima, after winning a legal case in that city in 66 AD, celebrated by rioting and terrorising the local Jews. Many of these Jews poured into Jerusalem, and the Zealots seized upon the opportunity and took the city, forcing the Roman garrison to surrender. This was the beginning of the Roman/Jewish war.

So the Zealots were originally based in Galilee, and Judas is described by Josephus as a "very clever Rabbi". Is it possible that some stories that have been ascribed to Jesus may have emanated from this Judas, by way of simple confusion? That perhaps *he* was the one who walked into the synagogues of Galilee and "astonished" the congregations with a fiery call to arms? And that the promises of worldly material gain for those who "leave their homes and families" would be achieved when they defeated the Romans? Consider this interesting miracle that Mark tells us Jesus performed when he came across a man possessed of an unclean spirit—

> "And when he saw Jesus afar off, he ran and worshipped him, and cried with a loud voice 'What have I to do with thee, Jesus, thou son of the most high God? I adjure thee by God, that thou torment me not.' For Jesus said unto him 'Come out of the man, thou unclean spirit.' And he asked him, 'What is thy name?' And he answered him, saying, *'My name is legion, for we are many.'* And he besought him much that he would not send them away out of the country. Now there was nigh unto the mountains a great herd of swine feeding, and all the devils besought him, saying 'Send us into the swine, that we may enter them.' And forthwith Jesus gave them leave, and the unclean spirits went out, and entered into the swine, and the herd ran violently down a steep place into the sea (they were about two thousand) and were choked." (Mk 5:6–13)

As demons do not carry passports it would seem bizarre that they should be concerned about being deported. If we take the possessed man to be the Holy Land possessed (occupied) by a Legion (Roman legions) of which there were about two thousand, the "miracle" immediately makes sense as just the kind of messianic promise cloaked in allegory that could have emanated from the Judas of Galilee school. The message sounds fairly clear—"Stick with me, boys, and we'll kick these Roman pigs out." Apart from their militarism, Josephus claimed their views were generally in accord with Pharisaism. I will return to the significance of these traces of zealotry later.

Naturally, other Hebrew scriptures and traditions have a lot to do with the construction of Jesus' personality, which helps to explain some strange behaviour on his part. Psalm 78:2 declares—

> "I will open my mouth in parables, I will utter dark sayings of old."

This was construed as a messianic prophecy. Accordingly, Jesus speaks in parables. In Mark 4, Jesus' disciples ask him to explain the meaning of one of the parables that he had delivered to the benighted public, and Jesus prefaces his answer with—

> "Unto you it is given to know the mystery of the kingdom of God—but unto them that are without, all these things are done in parables—That seeing they may see and not perceive; and hearing they may hear and not understand; lest at any time they should be converted, and their sins be forgiven them." (vs 11–12)

There can be no doubt that Mark is alleging that Jesus was *deliberately* disguising the meaning of what he was saying from his audience, for later we read—

> "...but without a parable spake he not unto them—and when they were alone, he expounded all things to his disciples." (v 34)

Why Jesus, who presumably was trying to save people and garner converts (which he would have needed to do if his career is the basis of Christianity!), should be so secretive can be understood if this trait was constructed from Isaiah 6, where we read—

> "I heard a voice of the Lord saying, 'Whom shall I send, and who will go for us?' Then said I, 'Here I am, send me!' And he said 'Go and tell these people, "Hear ye indeed, but understand not; and see ye indeed, but perceive not. Make the hearts of this people fat, and make their ears heavy, and shut their eyes; lest they see with their eyes, and hear with their ears, and

understand with their heart, and convert, and be healed.""" (vs 8–10)

What Mark wants his readers to believe, of course, is that Jesus is fulfilling this prophecy. This is a clear indication that there was a body of scriptures and traditions of what was expected of such a Messiah and much of Jesus' biography was built around them—even if this meant that some of his actions would fly in the face of a much more important purpose implicit in his having a ministry in the first place—that of converting people.

Matthew sensed the danger in Mark's reading of Isaiah and subtly sought to correct it. He has Jesus explaining to the disciples that the people can't understand his "parables" *because* their hearts have waxed gross, thereby throwing the blame for the communication problem onto the people for not understanding, and off Jesus for speaking too cryptically—indicating that Matthew captured the sense of Isaiah's words where Mark did not (see Mt 13:10–15). Notice the important point that the matter of what Jesus actually may have said (assuming the authors believed he existed) is secondary to the matter of him fulfilling prophecy.

Matthew's own enthusiasm for having Jesus fulfil prophecy trips him up as well, and creates many absurdities. For example, he has Jesus fulfilling prophecy by having him charge people not to tell anyone about his miracles. He quotes a piece from Isaiah, part of which includes the words—

> "...he shall not strive, nor cry, neither shall any man hear his voice in the streets." (Mt 12:19)

Matthew has Jesus fulfilling this by having him tell people whom he has healed to keep it to themselves. This would have been all very well if the best part of Matthew 23 were not filled with what could only have been a loud and ringing public denunciation of the Pharisees "ye murderers, serpents, ye generation of vipers etc" by the very same Jesus—in direct contravention of the Isaiahan prophecy.

There is good evidence that "Jesus" could not have made the famous apocalyptic speech (the "little apocalypse") attributed to him in Mark 13. It so happened that Caligula had sought to have the Legate of Syria set up a gigantic representation of Jupiter (with whom Caligula unsuccessfully tried to identify himself) in the Jerusalem temple, over the vehement objections of the pious. Although the Jewish Prince Agrippa managed to dissuade him from this action, many Jews were still apprehensive and were prepared to fight to prevent the crection of this statue—which Mark's Jesus refers to as "the abomination of desolation". The crisis peaked in 39–40 AD, but when Caligula was murdered in 41 AD, many Jews saw it as divine retribution. In reference to this event, Mark's Jesus says—

> "And except that the Lord had shortened those days, no flesh should be saved—but for the elect's sake whom he hath chosen, he hath shortened the days." (Mk 13–20)

It is interesting that this piece is written in the past tense. Jesus, of course, was supposed to have been executed in the time of Pilate, who was recalled in 36 AD—over four years before the death of Caligula. Pushing the possibility aside that Jesus may have foreseen the statue crisis and the sudden death of Caligula, the above text is evidence that the whole speech of Jesus in Mark 13 was developed from an oracle, which was supplemented as events and circumstances changed. The wording about the shortening of days comes from the Jewish apocryphal *Book of Enoch,* and must have been written after the demise of Caligula. The author of this oracle was either not familiar with the tradition of Jesus being crucified under Pilate, or the oracle was redacted into the text by someone who did not know that it referred to Caligula.

Drawing on Mark's "little apocalypse" but writing later, Luke has Jesus omitting any reference to the passing of the Caligula statue crisis—substituting it with a prediction by Jesus of the deportation of the Palestinian Jews which ensued from the Roman/Jewish war of 66/73 AD (see Lk 21:24). For evidence that Luke wrote the piece after the war, see Jesus' detailed description, in the form of a prediction, of the building of the wall of circumvallation by Titus' men during the siege of Jerusalem (Lk 19:43-4). With the passing of time, Jesus' ability to predict the future improves, and of course the siege of Jerusalem was far more important than the statue crisis. It's quite possible that Luke realised it was anachronous.

The gospel writers also made good use of Roman traditions and speeches. Augustus had commissioned Livy to write a history of Rome, to which the gospel writer would have had access. Romulus, the legendary founder of Rome, was the only Roman believed to be deified prior to Caesar. Livy reports on how Romulus appeared posthumously to his disciple Julius Proculus, telling him—

> "Go and tell the Romans that by Heaven's will my Rome shall be capital of the world...Let them learn to be soldiers. Let them know, and tell their children, that no power on Earth can stand against Roman arms." (Livy 1, 16)

After this Romulus disappears into the heavens. So the first commission by the Roman Founder-God was that the Romans should conquer the world. The next commission by Christ is that the world should be converted to the new Roman religion—Jesus appears posthumously to his disciples and commands—

> "Go ye into all the world and preach the gospel to every creature. He that believes and is baptised shall be saved, and he who does not shall be damned...so when the Lord had spoken to them, he was received up into heaven, and sat on the right hand of God." (Mk 16:15-9)

Mark also tells us that the sky darkened on Jesus' death—

> "And when the sixth hour was come, there was darkness over the whole land until the ninth hour." (Mk 15:33)

—just as the poets and historians had written of the dimmed sun after Caesar's death. The supernatural phenomena associated with Caesar's death were widely known, but perhaps because no one could remember the darkening of the sun at the time when Jesus was supposed to have died, the author limited himself to a three-hour occlusion. (Note: There was a total eclipse of the sun centring on Saudi Arabia on what would have been the 24th of November 29 AD, but no other occurred in the region until the year 46 AD. The first one is at least four months from Passover time, and the second is well after the time of Pilate; so we can rule out the eclipse theory as a natural explanation for the darkened sky.) Matthew, writing later, waxes more audacious. He tells us that after Jesus was crucified—

> "...the earth did quake, and the rocks rent; And the graves were opened; and many bodies of the saints that slept arose and came out of their graves after his resurrection, and went into the holy city and appeared unto many." (Mt 27:51-3)

Which faithfully echoes the mythic prodigies when Caesar was slain—

> "In the forum, and all about people's homes and the temples of the gods, dogs howled at night, and they say the silent dead walked, and earthquakes shook the city." (Ovid *Metamorphoses* XV, 796-9. *Inque foro circumque domos et templa deorum nocturnos ululasse canes umbrasque silentum erravisse ferunt motamque tremoribus urbem*)

The death of Christ cannot be seen to be less momentous than that of great Caesar. That the gospel writers should draw on Greco-Roman precedents is not only likely, it is *unlikely* that they would not, especially if the centrepiece of their religion came directly from the cult of *divus iulius*. Prior to Caesar, the brothers Gracchi had attempted to implement policies of a reformist nature. One well known saying of Jesus in particular seems to be a conscious paraphrasing of a famous speech on land reform made by the tribune of the people Tiberius Gracchus in 133 BC—

> "The beasts of the field and the birds of the air have their holes and hiding places, but the men who fight and die for Italy enjoy only the light and the air. Our generals urge their soldiers to fight for the graves and shrines of their ancestors. The appeal is idle and false, you cannot point to a paternal altar. You have no ancestral tomb. You fight and die to give wealth and luxury to others. You are called the masters of the world, but you do not have a foot of ground that you can call your own." (*Tiberius Gracchus*, Plutarch)"

And in Mt 8:20 (and Luke 9:58) we find Jesus saying of himself—

> "The foxes have holes, and the birds of the air have nests; but the Son of man hath not where to lay his head"

If we remove the italicised militaristic segment in the quote from Tiberius Gracchus we have the essence of the quote from Jesus. He has been substituted for the Roman soldiers, and the rest of the quote, just like the earlier one cited from Romulus, has been demilitarised. First comes the army, then comes the church.

Many of Jesus' miracles were concocted because, to enjoy status, he had to be able to do what previous gods had done, and more. These stories were obviously created some time after Paul, who clearly had no such conception of Christ. But healings were *de rigeur* for deities, and it was only a matter of time before they would make their way into the vita of the god. Exorcism was an article of faith, especially amongst the Jews, so Jesus has to be a master exorcist. Dionysus changed water into wine, so Jesus does, too. Dionysus (Bacchus), the god of the vine, managed this by enthusing the plant that absorbs water and transforms it into wine. Jesus does it by a snap of the fingers. When Aeneas and his comrades were threatened by a storm at sea, he prayed to the god Neptune who calmed the waters. Jesus similarly calms the sea, and even strolls across the top of it, etc.

The later gospel writers who built on Mark's foundation encountered some problems in attempting to construct a fuller biography for Jesus. Matthew, as noted, has gone to extraordinary lengths to fulfil prophecy, and helpfully points out when it has occurred. As Mark's gospel started with Jesus as a full-grown man, the question of where he came from and what he did for nigh on thirty years must have been increasingly asked. So to solve the problem of where Jesus came from, Matthew has provided him with an earthly birth, even if he tells us nothing of Jesus' life from early childhood till the start of his itinerant preaching career. He begins his story with an impressive genealogy, proving that Jesus is of royal blood in that he is descended, through his father Joseph, from King David. The tactic loses somewhat of its impact, though, when we get to the end of the chapter and learn that his mother Mary was supernaturally impregnated by the "Holy Spirit" before she and her betrothed Joseph had "come together". It is unlikely that a single writer would have written the two conflicting genealogies. The virgin birth story was created to compete with the ancient immaculately conceived gods like Romulus, Perseus, Horus etc., but more importantly the contemporary emperor Augustus himself. By retaining the Davidic heritage, Matthew has covered both heavenly and earthly options. He selects Bethlehem as the venue to fulfil prophecy—

> "And thou Bethlehem in the land of Judah, art not least amongst the princes of Judah—for out of thee shall come a governor, that shall rule my people Israel." (Mt 2:6)

This prophecy is from Micah 5:2, where it refers to David—held by tradition to have been born in Bethlehem. David was of course deceased when the Micahan text was penned, but it was believed that God would resurrect him at some future time to rule Israel (see e.g. Jeremiah 30:9). So Matthew has purloined the reference from David and given it to Jesus. He has Jesus born in the reign of Herod the Great who, when he learns from itinerant wise men that the Messiah has been born, commissions the Jewish chief priests to search out where that should be. They rifle through the scriptures, and come up with the town of Bethlehem, which information Herod then passes on to the wise men, telling them to report back with the exact location so that he himself can go and worship him. Learned though they were, the sagacious troika do not suspect his motives.

Their seeking of information from Herod on the venue for the Messiah's birth seems to have been unnecessary, as they depart from him and just continue to follow the herald-star which takes them to the correct destination anyway. They furtively worship the Christ child, and then God tells them through an angel not to report back to Herod, and they go home by a different route. Another angel appears to Joseph and tells him to flee with his wife and newborn boy to Egypt and to await further instructions, which he does.

When Herod finds out that he has been "mocked" by the wise men, he becomes "wroth" and sends his minions out to massacre all the children under two years of age in Bethlehem and "all the coasts thereof" (Mt 2:16). [Note: this slaughter, as might be expected, is not recorded by any historian and is generally dismissed. Its obvious literary source is the Genesis story of the slaughter of the innocents before the Israelites left Egypt, but it also mimics what was said of Augustus—"a public portent warned the Roman people some months before Augustus' birth that Nature was making ready to provide them with a king, and this caused the Senate such consternation that they issued a decree which forbade the rearing of any male child for a whole year" (Suet *Aug* 94). Again we see the true cause of concern—the Roman taboo of kings] Herod now dies, and yet another angel tells Joseph to take the boy Jesus from Egypt back to the land of Israel. All this complex activity took place so that the scripture might be fulfilled "out of Egypt have I called my son" (Mt 2:15). But this prophecy is cut from Hosea 11:1 where it refers to the Exodus of the Israelites from Egypt—

> "When Israel was a child, then I loved him, *and called my son out of Egypt.* As they called him, so they went from them, they sacrificed unto Balaam, and burned incense to graven images…" etc

That the Almighty should resort to such bizarre machinations to fulfil a six or seven word prophecy was totally lost on Luke, who has his Jesus being born after the institution of the census of Cyrenius which—as mentioned—took place in 6 AD. Luke's Holy family miss out on the trip to Egypt and back. And, as Herod the Great died in 4 BC—with Matthew's Jesus being born some time before that—we are left with something like a minimum ten year discrepancy between the two birth dates. Luke's version appears to have been inspired by Josephus' writings, wherein he provides information from around the time of the Cyrenian census that Luke used as a chronological hook to hang Jesus' birth on, lending credibility to the event by an impressive list of contemporary identities.

In fact, Luke's account of Jesus' roots and early childhood reads somewhat like a trumped up version of the early days of Josephus as recorded in that historian's autobiography—which Luke certainly had access to—intermingled with Judaic renditions of the auguries and phenomena pertaining to the birth of the *divi filius* Augustus. Luke tells us that Jesus was born in Bethlehem and provides him with an illustrious lineage from King David (which, incidentally, differs radically from Matthew's). Josephus wrote of himself—

> "My family is no ignoble one, tracing its descent far back to priestly ancestors." (The Life, 1)

—and goes on to give us a genealogy of several generations. He himself was born in the holy city of Jerusalem, and of course Luke's Jesus was born in the holy city of David—nearby Bethlehem. Josephus humbly says of himself—

> "Whilst still a small boy, about fourteen years old, I won universal applause for my love of letters; inasmuch that the chief priests and the leading men of the city used constantly to come to me for precise information on some particular in our ordinances." (*The Life,* 9)

And Luke tells us of the growing Jesus, who, at the tender age of twelve, was found to be missing. After three days of frantic searching his distraught parents finally locate him in the temple—

> "…sitting in the midst of doctors, both hearing them, and asking questions. And all that heard him were astonished at his understanding and answers." (Lk 2:46-7)

So the precocious youth conversing with and impressing learned elders comes from Josephus, but the disappearing act is from Augustus—

> "…one evening, the infant Augustus was placed by his nurse in his cradle on the ground floor, but had vanished by daybreak; at last a search party found him lying on the top of a lofty tower, his face turned toward the rising sun." (Suet *Aug* 94)

Luke has Jesus' mother Mary divinely impregnated by the Holy Spirit enlisting the angel Gabriel as proxy (Lk 1:26–38). Dio informs us that the mother of Augustus, Attia, held to the—

> "…emphatic declaration that the youth (the young Augustus) had been engendered by Apollo; for while sleeping once in his temple, she said, she thought she had intercourse with a serpent, and it was this that caused her at the end of her allotted time to bear a son." (Dio *RH,* XLV, 1)

Luke also found a Jewish literary source in the OT story of Samuel to embellish his portrait of Christ's birth. This prophet was born through divine beneficence (see 1 Sam 1:5–20): in similar fashion Luke's Jesus is born after an angelic announcement to his mother (Luke 1:35). What we know as the *magnificat*, delivered by Mary the mother of Jesus (Lk 1:45–55), is modelled on the poetic speech delivered by Hannah the mother of Samuel on the occasion of his birth (see 1 Sam 2:1–10). We further read of Samuel—

> "And the child grew on, and was in favour with both the Lord, and also with men." (1 Sam 2:26)

And Luke tells us of Jesus—

> "And Jesus increased in wisdom and stature, and in favour with God and man." (Lk 2:52)

Luke has detailed many other miraculous events pertaining to the birth of Jesus, and sought to tie the roots of John the Baptist and Jesus together. An angel tells Mary that her cousin Elizabeth is pregnant after having been barren (a common biblical theme, also said of Samuel's mother: see 1 Sam 1:5–20), so Mary goes to visit her in an unspecified city of Judea—

> "And it came to pass that, when Elizabeth heard the salutation of Mary, the babe leapt in her womb." (Lk 1:41)

John has intra-uterine awareness of Jesus' embryonic presence. Elizabeth then says to Mary—

> "Blessed art thou among women, and blessed is the fruit of thy womb. And whence is this to me, *that the mother of my Lord* should come to me?" (Lk 1:42-3)

The prescient Mary then delivers the aforementioned *magnificat*, and abides with Elizabeth three whole months, perhaps leaving before John the Baptist is born. When he is born, his father delivers the *benedictus*, part of which, in reference to his own son John, says—

> "And thou, child, shall be called the prophet of the Highest, for thou shalt go before the face of the Lord to prepare his way." (Lk 1:76)

And Luke informs us that when Jesus, years later, is baptised by this same John—

> "Heaven was opened, and the Holy Ghost descending in a bodily shape like a dove upon him, and a voice from Heaven, which said, 'Thou art my beloved son, in thee I am well pleased." (Lk 3:21-2)

John, here the master of ceremonies, must have witnessed this phenomenon. Yet later, after all these miraculous events and heavenly pronouncements, Luke tells us that John sends two emissaries to Jesus to ask—

> "Art thou he who should come? Or do we look for another?" (Lk 7:19)

Indicating that the Baptist had not really been paying much attention. If John could forget so easily, then small wonder it is that Clement still didn't seem to know the John the Baptist-as-herald-of-Jesus tradition by the end of the 1st century. What these fabulous and contradictory birth tales do demonstrate is that we have no reliable information on Jesus' birth at all, and these biblical accounts are made of whole cloth.

There is little ground for confidence that the teachings of Jesus that appear in the gospels of Matthew and Luke are his. Presumably drawing from an earlier document (not Mark's), both Matthew and Luke have Jesus delivering a major sermon—Matthew's on a mountain; Luke's on a plain. Much of the ingredients of this sermon can be found in the 52nd chapter of the earlier Jewish apocryphal *Secrets of Enoch,* which has a similar list of blessings (alternating with cursings). In chapter 44 we read of "Enoch" instructing his sons—

> "I swear unto you, my children, but I swear not by any oath, neither by heaven nor by earth, nor by any other creature that God created. The Lord said. 'There is no oath in me, nor injustice, but truth.' If there is no truth in men let them swear by the words 'Yea yea' or 'Nay nay'." (vs 1–3)

And Matthew's Jesus holds forth from the mount—

> "But I say unto you, swear not at all; neither by heaven, for it is God's throne; nor by earth, for it is his footstool; neither by Jerusalem, for it is the city of the great King, but let your com-

munication be, Yea yea, or Nay nay; for whatsoever is more
than these cometh from evil." (Mt 5:33-7)

The maxim was also widely used amongst the Essenes. We saw earlier that
Paul was either unaware of this teaching of Jesus, or paid it scant regard (see particularly Galatians 1:20). The golden rule which Jesus pronounces in Mt 7:12—

"Therefore all things whatsoever ye would that men should do
to you, do ye even so to them—for this is the Law and the
prophets"

—was not new to Judaism and is a paraphrase of a teaching attributed to Hillel the Babylonian who came to Jerusalem in the first century BC and founded a
school of liberal Pharisaism. He characterised Judaism as embodying the principal "do not unto others that which is hateful to thee", and said that the rest of the
Torah—which is what Jesus means here by "the Law"—was "mere commentary".
He admonishes his followers to "be of the disciples of Aaron, craving peace, pursuing peace, and loving human creatures". Those who take the time to read about
the activities of Aaron might find this surprising, but what Hillel was really doing
was employing the tools of tradition to promote civility and decency. As is almost
universally understood, variations of the golden rule appear in all the world's
great religions. Incidentally, some have pointed out that the Judaic formula is
superior to the Jesuine one, as doing something unto others that one would like
done to oneself does not allow that others' tastes might be different. But the Hil-
lelian one is similarly faulted, because others might actually like something that
one hates. A superior form would perhaps be "Do unto others as they would have
done unto them, but only if you want to".

This golden rule is not the only great saying falsely attributed to Jesus. Jump-
ing to John's gospel for a moment, we find Jesus entering the temple early one
morning—

"...and all the people came unto him, and he sat down, and
taught them." (Jn 8:2)

In the next verse, the "scribes and Pharisees" bring a woman caught in adul-
tery to him and ask him is she should, in accordance with the Law of Moses, be
stoned. Jesus, ignoring them, doodles on the ground with his finger. But the
Pharisees press him for an answer, and he comes out with the immortalised

maxim "Let he who is without sin cast the first stone", shaming his detractors into departing—

> "...and Jesus was left alone, and the woman standing in the midst, when Jesus had lifted himself up, and saw none but the woman, he said unto her, 'Woman, where are thine accusers?'" (vs 9–10)

She tells him they have gone, and he tells her to go and sin no more. But then we find that Jesus is *not* alone, as the very next verse begins—

> "Then spoke Jesus again unto them, saying..." (v 12)

Instant crowds? No, the homily is an insertion breaking the continuity between verses 2 and 12; it does not appear in the earliest codices and dates only from the 4th century. Some modern editions of the NT place the story in a footnote, others position it after Luke 21:28. It could be said this treasured saying is faulted too, incidentally, as it might encourage the self-righteous to throw stones.

A good example of how the gospel writers would shuffle a "saying" of Jesus around to suit their tastes is the use of the line from Psalm 118:26—"Blessed is he that cometh in the name of the Lord". Mark originally uses it as the cry of the crowd at Jesus' triumphal entry into Jerusalem (Mk 11:9). Matthew does too, but uses it again at the end of Jesus' vitriolic attack on the Pharisees, which took place *after* the triumphal entry, obviously referring to a time yet to come—

> "You shall not see me henceforth, *till* you say 'blessed is he that cometh in the name of the Lord'" (Mt 23:39).

Luke uses similar wording to Matthew's second reference but positions it earlier in Jesus' career, and again suggests a future fulfilment. Addressing himself to the city of Jerusalem from afar, Jesus says—

> "Ye shall not see me henceforth, until the time when ye shall say, 'Blessed is he that comes in the name of the Lord.'" (Lk 13:55)

However, in Luke this is fulfilled at Jesus' triumphal entry (19:38), and Jesus does not predict the use of the line at a still later date like the Jesus of Matthew does. The authenticity of this line is somewhat diminished by (a) its pre-existence in the Psalm, and by (b) the different usages of it in Mark, Matthew, and Luke.

Suffice it to say at this point that there was an abundance of existing lore, both oral and written, for the gospel writers to draw on to build the image of Jesus *qua* wise man and prophet. Now Luke has added some of his own material to the Passion story, which follows the gospel tendency of increasingly shunting the blame for the mistreatment of the Christ from the Romans (i.e. the Romans who killed Caesar) to the Jews as Christianity developed. The acrimony resulting from the Roman/Jewish war of 66–73 AD was probably the cause of this. Unlike the other gospels, Luke has Pilate send Jesus to (the Jewish) Herod Antipas, the tetrarch of Galilee—from where Jesus supposedly hailed. Pilate's motive for this, we are told, is that he wants to have no responsibility in the matter. We read that, in front of Antipas, the chief priests and scribes "vehemently accused him" (i.e. Jesus—and again we are given no indication of what the accusations are). In this version Herod's soldiers mock Jesus and array him in a "gorgeous robe". They then send him back to Pilate's domain where the screaming Jewish mob demands his crucifixion. Pilate suggests that he merely have Jesus scourged, then released. But the rabble become more insistent, so Pilate kowtows and delivers Jesus over to them *without the scourging and mocking by the Roman soldiers* reported in Mark. Thus are the Romans let off the hook for maltreating the deity.

A prophet indeed

We have already noted the later church belief that Jerusalem was destroyed as divine retribution for the killing of Christ. It may be that the works of Josephus helped this idea come about. When the Jewish rebellion broke out, Josephus had a command in Galilee. After being captured, he switched to the Roman side, later becoming a favoured state clerk and writing a history of that war—originally published between 75–79 AD. In this work he casts himself as a kind of latter-day Jeremiah, and writes of how he stood atop the walls of the temple exhorting the Jews to surrender and telling them that God has domiciled in Italy! He speaks of the might of Rome—

> "For what is there of the world that has escaped the Romans, save maybe some place useless through heat or cold? Fortune, indeed, has from all quarters passed over to them, and God, who does the round of the nations, bringing to each in turn the rod of empire, *is now settled in Italy*." (*BJ*, V, 366-7)

Under a hail of missiles he decries—

> "Ah, miserable wretches, unmindful of your own true allies, would you make war on the Romans with arms and might of hand? (...) for myself, I shudder at recounting the works of God to unworthy ears; yet listen, *that you may learn that you are warring not against the Romans only, but also against God."* (*BJ*, V, 376, 378)

After telling them that their sins are the cause of their misfortunes, he points out the road to salvation—

> "Yet a way of salvation is still left to you, if you will—and the Deity is easily reconciled to such as confess and repent. Oh iron-hearted men! Fling away your weapons, take compassion on your country even now tottering to its fall, turn from your wicked ways and behold the beauty of what you are betraying—What a city! What a temple! What precious nations' gifts!" (*BJ*, V, 415-6)

God will forgive you if you stop fighting the Romans. And Matthew's Jesus, curiously enough, seems to be in full accord. Just prior to Jesus predicting the destruction of the Jerusalem temple by the Romans, Matthew has him delivering a long and vitriolic denunciation of the "scribes and Pharisees". His last accusation against them—in a list of crimes beginning with the traditional murder of Abel by Cain—is the responsibility for killing a Jew accused of being a Roman agent just prior to the outbreak of the war. Jesus complains that he has sent them (here Jesus presents himself as the eternal God) "prophets and wise men and scribes" whom they have variously crucified, scourged and persecuted—

> "...(so) that upon you may come all the righteous blood shed upon the earth, from the blood of righteous Abel unto the blood of Zacharias the son of Barachias whom ye slew between the temple and the altar. Verily I say unto you, all these things shall come upon this generation" (Matt 23:34-6)

Shortly before the war began, the Zealots had sought the execution of a certain "Zacharias, the son of Baruch" because they thought he was going to betray their insurrectionary intentions to the Romans. They held a tribunal in the temple, inviting a panel of seventy eminent citizens to adjudicate. When the Zealots realised that the dignitaries were not satisfied that they had established their case against the arraigned man, "…two of the boldest of them *fell upon Zacharias in the middle of the temple and slew him*" (see *BJ*, IV 334–343).

Christians usually assume this to be a reference to the slaying of the traditional prophet "Zechariah, the son of Berechiah", supposedly contemporary with Darius. But Jesus is obviously linking his accusation to the imminent destruction of the temple, not to an event that could only have occurred centuries earlier. The speech makes Matthew's Jesus sound like a Roman sympathiser. And if it is not enough that Christ here appears to be anachronistically mimicking Josephus, Josephus, for his part, terminates his plea for the Jews to surrender to Rome by offering himself as a Christ-like sacrifice—

> "I know that I have a mother, a wife, a not ignoble family, and an ancient and illustrious house involved in these perils; and maybe you think that it is on their behalf that my advice is offered. *Slay them, take my blood as the price of your own salvation, I too am prepared to die, if my death will lead to your returning to a sound mind!*" (*BJ*, V, 419)

It is not hard to see where the developing church may have got the idea that the destruction of Jerusalem was God's vengeance. There is a pattern here. The record of Jesus' early career in the gospels seems to contain elements that stem from the anti-Roman Zealot movement based in Galilee, e.g. the nationalist pig exorcism at Mk 5:6–13 or such texts as Matt 10:34 "Think not that I am come to send peace on earth, I come not to send peace but a sword". Josephus begins his war career with a command in Galilee. Justus of Tiberias accused Josephus of stirring up nationalist fervour there. Josephus later switches sides. Jesus also appears to switch sides, and condemns the Zealots for killing a Roman agent (well after his own time, of course)! Josephus offers his own life as a sacrifice to prevent the destruction of the temple: Jesus laments that he (himself) could have saved Jerusalem, *and* the temple. His "prediction" of its destruction follows immediately upon his complaint about the killing of Zacharias and his prophetic lament over the fate of Jerusalem—

> "O Jerusalem Jerusalem, thou that killest the prophets, and stonest them that are sent unto thee. How often would I have gathered thy children together as a hen gathereth her chickens under her wings, and ye would not! Behold, your house is left unto you desolate." (Matt 23:37-8)

Jesus is here bewailing that Jerusalem, for its sins, is to be destroyed by Rome, an eventuality that he regretfully endorses, just like Josephus does. If we step back and look at the broad picture here we can note that by the end of the book of Acts, Paul is in Rome. The Catholic Church claims Peter as the first bishop of Rome. Amongst the portents that Josephus described just prior to the fall of Jerusalem was a supernatural ruckus issuing from the back of the temple and a noise as "of a host" exclaiming "Let's get out of here!" (*BJ,* VI 299–300) The gods certainly did quit Jerusalem, and they went directly to Rome, just as assuredly as the temple Menorah was carried there for the triumphal procession after the war. And Jesus Christ is still firmly ensconced in the eternal city today. Great Caesar's Ghost didn't take long to find its way back home.

The view, later developed, that Rome was fulfilling the will of God in destroying Jerusalem is clearly enunciated by Jesus. Clement, as we saw, knew no such tradition, but even Mark's early Jesus did. In his twelfth chapter, Jesus tells a parable of a husbandman who let out a vineyard. When it came time to gather the grapes, he sent emissaries to the tenants, who beat the envoys and sent them away "shamefully treated". The longsuffering husbandman then decides to send his "well-beloved son" (obviously Jesus), whom he is sure they will respect.

But they don't. They decide they want the inheritance themselves, so they "took him, and killed him, and cast him out of the vineyard." Mark's Jesus then posits and answers the question—

> "What shall the Lord of the vineyard do? He shall come and
> kill those murderers, and give the vineyard unto others."

There can be little doubt that "Jesus" is referring to his own execution and the later Roman destruction of Jerusalem as punishment for it. Does this mean that Rome is taking the covenant, the "vineyard", from the Jews and handing it to the Christians? In complete contrast to the Jewish nationalist/anti-Roman spirit of the pig miracle, the "Messiah" now appears to have switched sides—just like Josephus. Matthew has developed this theme more explicitly, where we find "Jesus" again addressing the notorious chief priests and Pharisees. Right after his version of the parable of the vineyard—

> "Jesus said unto them, 'Did you never read in the scriptures,
> the stone which the builders rejected has become the head of
> the corner—This is the Lord's doing, and it is marvellous in
> your eyes? *Therefore I say unto you, the Kingdom of God shall be
> taken from you and given to a nation bringing forth the fruits*

thereof. And whoever shall fall on this stone shall be broken, but on whomsoever it shall fall, it will grind him to powder.' And when the chief priests and Pharisees had heard his parable, they perceived that he spoke of them." (Mt 21:42-5)

The stone, of course, is he—Jesus. The chief priests and Pharisees reject him by killing him; the Kingdom of God is removed from Jerusalem to Rome after the Roman armies—acting as God's agents—crush the city in question. The italicised section in the text above is clearly an interpolation, either by "Matthew" or a later hand, as removing it delivers continuity between the verses for and aft. Confirmation of the fiddling hand is provided by comparing it with Mark's Jesus, who reportedly said—

> "'The stone which the builders rejected has become the head of the corner, this is the Lord's doing, and it is marvellous in your eyes?' Then they sought to lay hands on him...etc" (Mk 12:10–12)

And also Luke's version, where we read that Jesus says—

> "What is this then that is written, The stone which the builders rejected is become the head of the corner? Whosoever shall fall upon that stone shall be broken, but on whomsoever it shall fall, it will grind him to powder." (Lk 20:17-8)

Further proof of the precise intent of the Matthean interpolation is furnished in his very next chapter. "Jesus" again speaks in parables—

> "The Kingdom of heaven is like unto a certain King, which made a marriage for his son, and sent forth his servants to call them that were bidden to the wedding, and they would not come. Again, he sent forth other servants, saying, 'Tell them which are bidden, Behold, I have prepared my dinner—my oxen and my fatlings are killed, and all things are ready—come unto the marriage'. But they made light of it, and went their ways, one to his farm, another to his merchandise. *And the remnant took his servants, and treated them spitefully, and slew them. But when the king heard thereof, he was wroth—And he sent forth his armies and destroyed those murderers and burnt up their city.* Then he said to his servants, 'The wedding is ready, but they which were bidden were not worthy. Go ye therefore

into the highways, and as many as ye shall find, bid to the marriage.'" (Mt 22:1–9)

The servants proceed to round up some guests, but when the king finds a man amongst them not wearing a garment, he has him cast into utter darkness (the poor soul had been dragged in from the street unawares). Those who believe that "Jesus" taught a coherent philosophy can forget about the doctrines of salvation by works *and* universal grace for the nonce, as the point of this parable is that the king—Jesus—is arbitrarily selective about whom he allows into his Kingdom, for "many are called, but few are chosen" (see v 14).

The italicised section in the text from Matthew quoted above is an interpolation serving the same purpose as the one dealing with the builder's stone. There *was* no remnant, all those originally invited to the wedding went about their own business. There is nothing here to suggest that the invited guests were not from the king's own city, which he would hardly burn down in the middle of wedding preparations. The king in the inserted piece, of course, is Rome—and the incinerated city is Jerusalem. Again the interpolation is proven by comparing Luke's version where, when the equivalent of the king (in this case, the master of the house) learns that the invitees refuse to come, we read—

> "Then the master of the house, being angry, said to the servants, 'Go out quickly into the streets and lanes of the city, and bring hither the poor, and the maimed, and the blind.'" (Lk 14:21)

No burning of the city here. The continuity in Luke exposes the Rome-as-God's-agent interpolation in Matthew. Luke's parable, incidentally, is employed to illustrate that Jesus is for the meek and lowly, the underdogs, not for the high and mighty. The idea that "many are called, but few are chosen" does not enter the picture. This is in keeping with Luke's Jesus, who is almost consistently anti-rich. What the two parables further indicate is that the gospel writers must have drawn from the corpus of generic stories and traditions and altered them for their own particular propaganda purposes. Worth noting is that if the original form of the parable, whatever it may have been, was believed to have issued from the mouth of Jesus, then the gospel writers have shown little respect for the actual words of the man. Just as today, they were all trying to make Jesus say what they wanted him to say, within the strictures of acceptability.

On a different note, a few words should be said about the gospel of John, which differs radically from the synoptics. The author has not even attempted to follow the pattern of the other gospels when constructing his own pre-Passion career for Jesus. Although he has supplemented and altered aspects of the Passion story, *he has left the basic details intact*—an indication of its pre-eminent status. The Passion accounts, of course, are the most detailed sections in all the gospels—with a concentration on time and action.

As John's gospel was written late and at a time of animosity between church and synagogue, it tends to portray "the Jews" as inherently evil. Jesus is the Son of Light walking amongst the Children of Darkness, the Jews. The gospel has some major singularities. Jesus' miracles have been vastly improved in general quality *but he does no exorcisms at all;* possibly because the author is not interested in appealing to the Jews, many of whom expected exorcism from a messiah. The career of Jesus spans two to three years, unlike the synoptics' one year; Jesus attacks the merchants in the temple with a "scourge of small cords" at his first Jerusalem Passover. No sudden loss of temper here, the action is clearly premeditated—Jesus sits down and patiently makes the weapon (Jn 2:15)! Forget the famous Sermon on the Mount, John did—it's not in his gospel.

John the Baptist doesn't baptise John's Jesus, who walks tallest of the four NT Jesuses. As a matter of fact the Baptist even says of his relationship to Jesus "He must increase, but I must decrease" (Jn 3:30). John's Baptist is far more prescient than Luke's Baptist, who found it necessary to send envoys out to ask Jesus the immortal question "Art thou he who should come? Or do we search for another?"

Unlike in the synoptics, *John's Jesus baptises—*

> "After these things came Jesus and his disciples into the land of
> Judea; and there he tarried with them, and baptised." (Jn 3:22)

So the author of John has deleted John the Baptist's prestigious baptism of Jesus, made the Baptist predict his own downward slide whilst Jesus' star ascends, and capped it all off by obliterating any specialness on the Baptist's part by having Jesus casually performing the baptismal rite as well (a later interpolator tries to deny this). So starting with Mark's scant pre-Passion Jesuine biography, we see the later writers providing more details and filling in the holes in the story. Jesus walks taller and taller, and is a superlative divinity by the time of John's writing. As Jesus takes on more historical meat, his relationship with "the Jews" deteriorates as the later gospel writers, *seeking to explain why Jesus was executed and to make the deicide credible,* had to portray the Jewish authorities as being implacably hostile to Jesus. And this is the real reason why we are never given specifics of the charges laid against him; it is sufficient for us to believe that he was "vehemently accused" by "false witnesses".

In summation, the pre-Passion biography of the life of Jesus seems to have evolved over a period of time to fulfil the sect's messianic expectations, and also in response to questions asked about his earthly existence. Signs and wonders were added for the vulgar. Snatches of text reveal there were conflicting political considerations involved as well. So we have finished up with a Jesus who is at once a wonder-worker, and a man who refuses to give signs of his divinity. A master exorcist, and a man who does no exorcisms at all. A pious preacher of righteousness, and an advocate and harbinger of vengeance. A Jewish Zealot/ nationalist, and a prophet of Roman supremacy. An advocate of forgiveness, as well as eternal damnation! This is what partisans of a historical Jesus call his "uninventable" character. The gospels as we know them are too chaotic and contradictory to have been the starting point of Christianity. Rather, it appears that the 2nd century church created the gospel Jesus.

Ramifications

When beggars die there are no comets seen,
but the heavens themselves blaze forth the death of princes

Tradition has it that Jesus, on his way to Golgotha, asked a certain cobbler named Ahasueris for a cup of water, and was refused. Ahasueris became the wandering Jew who, for his rejection of Jesus, is doomed to roam the earth until the Second Coming. In most versions of the traditon Ahasueris is an unreconstructed Jew clinging to his ancient beliefs, but in others he converted to Christianity long ago, but still has to live on till Jesus returns. Whatever the version, he has an important role to play—he is an eyewitness to the crucifixion, bearing testimony to its truth. This myth is important because even today, the mainstream rabbinic view of Jesus is that he did exist, but was not the Messiah. In this way many contemporary Jews play their part in the role of Ahasueris by bearing testimony to Jesus' historicity, but this testimony cannot be trusted.

It is easy to see how it developed that the rabbis today generally don't deny the existence of Jesus. It is certainly not because they have any particular inside information on the matter. Modern Judaism largely defines itself against Christianity. From the Judaic point of view it is *the Christian claim of the divinity of Jesus* that is the bone of contention, not whether he existed or not. This is one reason why so many people today don't doubt the existence of Jesus—it seems irrelevant—a somewhat damning thing to say about the supposed founder of one of the world's greatest religions. It must be remembered that Jesus took quite some time to become widely famed. As time passed by, and more and more people embraced Christianity, the existence of a man with the common name of Jesus would hardly have been seen as a difficulty.

When our gospels became widely extant, the vagueness of the historical setting of Jesus would have deflected the question of whether he had existed. All the people mentioned in the gospels (those who really existed) were dead and gone; Jerusalem had been overthrown. How could it ever be proven, for example, that there was never a man called Jesus wandering around preaching in the back blocks of Palestine with a band of men? It hardly sounds like an impossibility.

And, after Christianity became the state religion of Rome and the Jews started to feel the heel of Christian dominance, for a Jew to suggest that Jesus never existed would be seen as an easy way for him to dodge the issue of his godhead, and could be construed as a sign of perfidy. However, there are no authentic references to the life of the gospel Jesus from his contemporaries. The accusation of the "argument from silence" in this case is a red herring. It is not the lack of references to Jesus by contemporaries that consign him to the myth tray, rather that the earliest correspondences of Christianity are irreconcilable with the figure in the gospels.

The Christian myth that a Jew should bear witness to the truth of the crucifixion of Christ is indicative of the bizarre relationship between Judaism and Christianity. Judas Iscariot is reviled as the betrayer of Jesus, yet according to the Christian's credo, that very betrayal and execution leads to his own salvation. Judas can really only be culpable if his actions brought about Jesus' death, but without that atoning death the Christian would be damned—by his own logic. The earnest Christian must be content to believe that if Jesus had died peacefully in his sleep at an advanced age all salvation plans would have been cancelled. This is why the bewailing of Jesus' murder in the Thessalonian epistle jars against the spirit of Paul's carefully fabricated cosmology.

Such a belief system—that of the professing Christian—necessitates a kind of schizoid attitude towards the character Judas, and this carries over into the Christian attitude towards Judaism, which is touted as the only "true" religion prior to the advent of Christianity. The central notion that God was here amongst us and was murdered is singular amongst the great religions of the world today. Jungians might choose to cite the crucified God as an "archetype", but if that's the case, it is not a universal one. The Koran, for its part, claims that Jesus was never crucified—

> "And their saying: Surely we have killed the Messiah, Isa son of Marium, the apostle of Allah. They did not kill him nor did they crucify him, but it appeared to them so (like Isa) and most surely those who differ therein are only in a doubt about it; they have no knowledge respecting it, but only follow a conjecture, and they certainly killed him not." (Sutra 4:157)

In the Koran, Jesus (Isa) is subtly damned with faint praise: He is a mighty apostle of Allah, for sure, but Mohammed is mightier. In the meantime, the very centrepiece of Christianity—the great universal sin-expiating sacrifice—has been quietly shunted aside. The crucified god is of little import to the Hindus; they have so many divinities and eschatologies that Christ blends inconspicuously into their cosmic wallpaper. Buddhists also seem to have gotten along without the archetype. Their deity, whose biography is as ethereal as that of Jesus, is content to quietly wax increasingly rotund while contemplating his own insignificance in the great scheme of things.

But if this crucified god "archetype" was created, or revitalised, by a religion that rode on the back of the Caesar tragedy, we have to consider how much the Western unconscious has been affected by the inculcation of a concept of God which originated as a reflection of Roman politics. The life and death of Julius Caesar heralded the end of the old Republic, and Caesar was far more dangerous to the republicans as a martyred god than he would have been had he died of old age or even been killed on the Parthian battlefield. But his deification, combined with the fact that his chosen heir, Octavian, emerged triumphant from the civil wars to become Augustus—now son of the Founder/God and first official emperor of Rome, signalled the end of the Republic and the birth of a new age, replete with a new concept of God. The greatest surviving proof that Caesar created a new era stares us in the face every time we look at a calendar. There the new God and the Son of that God are immortalised—just as Jupiter promised they would be—in the names of July and August, the only two divinised humans to have survived successive attempts to change the calendar instituted by Julius himself.

The erstwhile Octavian was prudent enough to be mindful of what led to the murder of his divine sire, and paid lip service to the old traditions, ensuring that all his decisions and decrees were ostensibly arrived at in concert with the Senate. When the civil wars were finally over he proclaimed the restoration of the Republic. In gratitude the Senate showered him with oak leaves and lauded him as *augustus* and *princeps*. Ironically, this event in itself flagged that the Republic was a thing of the past. Although the Senate was restored, its true status had been undermined and it was effectively enfeebled. The people had become accustomed to being ruled by an Imperator, and this is the basis of my suggestion that this transition and evolution in the psyche of Roman citizens, and more particularly the provincial people, prepared the table for Christian monotheism.

If Jesus Christ is the ghost of Julius Caesar it is not surprising that once he was admitted to the Roman pantheon he would shoulder all the other gods off their clouds. The Roman Senate, for all its faults, was the earthly equivalent of polytheism, no man was supposed to have total power. The rise of absolutism that came with Caesar is the earthly parallel of monotheism, the heavens had to follow suit. As the celestial realms took on more the form of the Imperium, the old religions became increasingly irrelevant culturally. There is an adage, "what isn't illegal is compulsory, and what isn't compulsory is illegal". Once Christianity became the largest religion, it would not be long before it became the sole religion. Ultimately, Christ did not become the enduring single Western God in a free spiritual market, but rather by political imposition for purposes of uniting the Roman world. This may have been what Caesar had in mind when he set about creating the Imperial cult.

Aristotle wrote in his *Politics*—

> "If there exists in a state an individual so pre-eminent in virtue
> that neither the virtue nor the political capacity of all the other
> citizens is comparable with his…such a man should be rated as
> a god amongst men".

It is in this context that the deification of Caesar must be seen. Unlike the later Caesars, Julius did not inherit his title as a god, he earned it and it was conferred on him. Even his most ardent detractors cannot deny his essential greatness and magnanimity unprecedented in strongmen in the annals of Rome, and it is almost universally conceded that this, embodied in his *clementia,* was instrumental in bringing about his downfall. That clemency was destroyed by the circumstances and aftermath of his murder, and was never really seen again in the ancient world. What hope was there for reconciliation when the great reconciler himself had been slain by the men he had pardoned and promoted? There was only one way for things to go. The infamous proscriptions returned with a vengeance during the civil war—the Second Triumvirate reverted to the murderous policy of Sulla, the very policy that Caesar had faithfully sworn to bury.

Augustus, by adopting the name of Caesar as was his right, provided much of the world with the ersatz title for King which has existed right till the 20th century of the Caesarian era—Kaiser, Czar, Cesarz, Cisar, Car and even the Arabic Qaysar. Some "good emperors" followed the two founding Caesars, but the lunacy of a Caligula and a Nero made a lampoon of the idea of the divine emperor. Much better to set the monarch in a realm where he can remain untainted by the earthly failings of the Caesars—hence the celestial Christ gradually superseded the earthly Caesar.

But for Christ to step into the shoes of Caesar, he had to mirror his fate. The reader will recall that in all the authentic pre-gospel Christian writings, from Paul through to Clement, Christ is *never* referred to as a "king" or the "King of the Jews" (1 Timothy is pseudo-Pauline). For over sixty years the Christian writers, in all their voluminous correspondence, never mention it. Nor is there ever any suggestion in their writings that Jesus thought he was the King of the Jews, or claimed to be such, or was thought to be such, or was falsely accused of trying to usurp such a position. There is no trace in their early letters of any attempt to reconcile this issue (*viz*—did he claim to be the *king*, or not?). We find no "if only's" nor "what ifs", no rationalisations, no disclaimers—*yet this very theme is central to the gospels' Passion drama,* wherein Jesus' royal pretensions are the basis for Pilate ordering his execution. The cry of the crowd "We have no king but Caesar!" could not be more explicit, nor ironic—and all the gospels have this very "accusation" superscribed on Christ's cross—"The King of the Jews" (Mk 15:26; Mt 27:37; Lk 23:38; Jn 19:19). This has been directly borrowed from the deicide of Caesar, and I have presented evidence that, not only were the early Christians oblivious to all this, their writings and quietistic admonitions positively exclude its authenticity. This *political* drama of the death of Christ appears to have been have been concocted somewhere between 100 to 140 AD. Christian apocryphal tradition even ascribes all manner of ghastly fates to those connected with the murder of Christ—Pilate, Caiaphas, the various Herods, etc—justly echoing what was said of the assassins of Caesar—

> "But that great divine power or genius, which had watched over him (Caesar) and helped him in his life, even after his death remained active as an avenger of his murder, pursuing and tracking down the culprits over every land and sea until not one of them was left, and visiting with retribution all, without exception, who were in any way concerned either with the death itself or with the planning of it." (Plut, *Life of JC*, 69)

Thus the story of the death of Christ eclipsed that of Caesar's by stealing all his thunder. The figure of Jesus Christ, standing at the crossroads of history, obscures the events that took place in Rome just prior to his time setting, and diverts our attention into Hebrew history as if the civilisations of Greece and Rome had never existed. It masks the story of Julius Caesar and the agonised death of the old order. This is probably the reason why the deification of Julius Caesar is not well known, and why it is generally thought that the Imperial cult began with Augustus. In this sense, then, the story of the Passion of Christ can justly be called the *foundation myth* of the Roman Empire.

The image of the man who would be King being brought down by jealous adversaries symbolised by an aspiring Brutus is so deeply embedded in Western culture that we fail to see how it shaped our religion. It famously appears in the form of knives and togas in political cartoons every time there is a whiff of a palace revolution anywhere. It has echoed down through the ages since the fateful Ides of March and uncannily manifested in Washington D.C. on that other Good Friday of April 14 1865 in the balcony of the Ford theatre, when the unsuspecting audience imagined they heard the assassin of Abraham Lincoln cry *sic semper tyrannis* as he crashed to the stage floor. Both the father and brother of John Wilkes Booth bore the name of Junius Brutus.

Gibbon noted that the faithful recorders of history would never allow Julius Caesar's faulted biography to become the object of eternal devotion. But, ironically enough, the phantasmal hero of the New Testament—Jesus of Nazareth—is similarly faulted, and falls far short of the perfect character he is so often touted to be. This picture of Jesus, promoted by mainstream Christianity, is not something easily gleaned from the accounts we have of his supposed life and teachings. A friendly and high-minded gospel Jesus can only be extracted by ignoring many of his reputed sayings and actions. Free of preconceptions, only a confused, contradictory and generally unedifying character can be construed from the scriptures. This stands to reason, as it is a difficult task to write the vita of a deity without affronting normal human sentiments. What are we to make of Jesus' saying to his mother, "Woman, what have I to do with thee?" (Jn 2:4); or his berating of the Pharisee, at whose dinner table he was a guest, for not anointing his head and feet on entrance (Lk 7:36–46)? Where does this leave his much-vaunted egalitarian disposition? His opinion of the efficacy of prayer as espoused at Luke 18:1–7, wherein he likens God to a corrupt magistrate, is little short of abhorrent. It must be remembered that much of the acrimony that suffuses the pronouncements of the gospel Jesus, in particular Matthew's character, is reflective of controversies and hostilities that raged within the 2nd century church when the gospels were being written. Hence the idealised "meta-Jesus" of Christianity is a far greater soul than the gospel one. This is hardly a controversial opinion; it is the basis for why the German theologian Rudolf Bultmann considered it imperative to divorce the "Christ of faith" from the "Jesus of history".

In the meantime the deity Jesus Christ, just like his formulaic predecessor Attis, continues to die and resurrect every year. But a creed that grew to be as great as did Christianity could not have come into being had there not been a truly remarkable man hailed as a god treacherously betrayed and murdered right here on earth—an event so momentous as to shake the ground, wake the dead and dim the sun.

That man was Julius Caesar.

Afterword

This book is a reprint of my book *Et tu Judas? Then Fall Jesus!* published in 1992. I have sought to correct some of the more egregious errors and clarify some arguments on the historicity of Christ. In 2001 I became aware of the work of Francesco Carotta in Germany. He has published articles and books which express some similar ideas to mine. It is not the purpose of the present book to discuss Mr Carotta's theories, this can be done in another place. Mr Carotta is publishing an English version of his work in 2004.

Gary Courtney, 2004.

Bibliography

APPIAN, *Roman History,* Bynneman's Ed., 1956.

BAILEY, Cyril, *Religion in Virgil,* Clarendon Press, 1935.

BARROW, R.H., *The Romans,* Penguin, 1968.

CANNADINE & PRICE, *Rituals of Royalty,* Cambridge Uni. Press, 1987.

COHN, Haim, *The Trial and Death of Jesus,* London, 1972.

DIMONT, Max I., *Jews, God, and History,* New American Library, 1962.

DION, Cassius, *Roman History,* Loeb Classical Lib., trans. E. Gary, 1914.

EPSTEIN, Isadore, *Judaism,* Penguin, 1959.

FRAZER, J.G., *The Golden Bough*, MacMillan & Co., 1967.

GARDNER, Martin, *Fads & Fallacies,* Dover Publications, 1952.

GRANT, F.C., *The Gospels—Their Origin and their Growth*, London, 1959.

GRANT, Michael, *Julius Caesar,* Weidenfeld & Nicholson, London, 1969.

JAMES, M.R., *Apocryphal New Testament*, Clarendon Press, Oxford, 1926.

JEWETT, Robert, *Dating Paul's Life,* S.C.M. Press, 1979.

JOSEPHUS, Flavius, *Antiquities of the Jews*, Loeb Classical Library.

JOSEPHUS, Flavius, *The Jewish War,* Loeb Classical Library.

LEVINE, Lee, *Caesarea under Roman Rule,* Brill, 1975.

MACCOBY, Hyam, *Revolution in Judaea,* Ocean Books, London, 1973.

MORGENSON, Greg, *God is a Trauma*, Spring Publications, Dallas, 1989.

PHILOSTRATUS, *Life of Apollonius of Tyana*, Loeb Classical Library. Brill,

PLUTARCH, *Lives*, Loeb Classical Library.

ROBERTSON, J.M., *Pagan Christs*, Dorset Press, N.Y., reprint 1966.

SCHONFIELD, Hugh, *The Passover Plot*, Element Books, reprint 1985.

SEVENSTER, J.N., *Paul and Seneca*, Brill, 1961.

SHAKESPEARE, W., *The Tragedy of Julius Caesar*.

SUETONIUS, *The Twelve Caesars*, Penguin, 1983.

WEINSTOCK, S., *Divus Julius*, Clarendon Press, Oxford, 1971.

WELLS, G.A., *The Jesus of the Early Christians*, London 1971.

WINTER, Paul, *On the Trial of Jesus*, Berlin, 1961.

0-595-32868-7

Made in the USA
Lexington, KY
21 July 2013